GHOSTLY ENCOUNTERS

Dennis Waskul *with* Michele Waskul

Ghostly Encounters

THE HAUNTINGS OF EVERYDAY LIFE

TEMPLE UNIVERSITY PRESS
Philadelphia • *Rome* • *Tokyo*

TEMPLE UNIVERSITY PRESS
Philadelphia, Pennsylvania 19122
www.temple.edu/tempress

Photographs by Dennis Waskul

Library of Congress Cataloging-in-Publication Data

Names: Waskul, Dennis D., 1969– author.
Title: Ghostly encounters : the hauntings of everyday life / Dennis Waskul,
  with Michele Waskul.
Description: Philadelphia : Temple University Press, 2016. | Includes
  bibliographical references and index.
Identifiers: LCCN 2015040034 | ISBN 9781439912881 (cloth: alk. paper) |
  ISBN 9781439912898 (paper: alk. paper) | ISBN 9781439912904 (e-book)
Subjects: LCSH: Ghosts. | Parapsychology.
Classification: LCC BF1461 .W39 2016 | DDC 133.1—dc23
LC record available at http://lccn.loc.gov/2015040034

Printed in the United States of America

9 8 7 6 5 4 3 2 1

To all of us restless spirits

CONTENTS

PREFACE

The content of this book is the product of typical academic labor and reflexive ethnographic fieldwork. That is, we explore reported experiences with ghosts and hauntings through interviews, firsthand written accounts of uncanny occurrences, historical research, and—whenever possible—visits to places where ghosts are said to haunt. We relate what we have learned to existing literature in the social sciences and humanities, cognizant that our audience is not made up of scholars and academics alone.

Certainly, as is appropriate and expected, the customary product of academic labor is typically in dedicated service to disciplinary interests. But academic labor is all about gathering information, discovering, making sense of what is found, and—ultimately—conveying what is learned to an audience. These same academic tools and skills can be employed to service general interests, as well as purely academic ones, and it is not always necessary to maintain a sharp divide between the two. Academic labor can be gainfully conducted without the use of extensive theory, an abundance of jargon, and dreary technical writing. *Ghostly Encounters*, which seeks to achieve this objective, is intended primarily to service general interests, especially for readers who wish to better understand how people experience ghosts in everyday life, characteristics of hauntings, and forms of ghostly experiences; what these encounters mean to people; and the consequences thereof. At the same time, scholars, particularly ethnographers, sociologists, social psychologists, cultural anthropologists, and folklorists, will find an adequate intellectual meal to digest.

Ghostly Encounters is, as stated, a reflexive ethnography. While ethnography means many things to many people, at a bare minimum it entails fieldwork and the use of observational data. Beyond that, ethnographers are methodologically promiscuous, and we are no exception. We collected data using multiple methods and gathered information from whatever reliable source we could find. (See the Appendix for more details on our methods and data.) Ethnography also means the construction of unique kinds of texts—highly descriptive, rich in detail—and frequently includes a strategic use of purposive storytelling to illustrate important dynamics that are contextualized in the lived experiences of people. For these reasons, ethnographic texts often contain significantly more drama than other genres of academic writing; hence, at times portions of ethnographic texts can read like a novel, but while novels are built from imagination, ethnographic narratives are built from a process of careful data collection. As a *reflexive* ethnography, this book includes our firsthand experiences alongside and interwoven with those that were reported by and observed among the participants in this study. Although *Ghostly Encounters* is a product of Michele's and my collaborative efforts—we jointly gathered data and conducted the analysis—I wrote the text, and it therefore reflects my first-person perspective.

The collection, analysis, and reporting of data were carried out with the accuracy and precision that are necessary to any academic study. Above and beyond the challenge of this objective, early in the data collection process certain discoveries compelled me to fundamentally rethink the research, reconsider the content of the book, and ultimately rearrange how I re-present what we learned along the way. For example, although the experiences people shared were always perplexing and uncanny—I expected this and found the proverbial "things that go bump in the night," along with the hackneyed monster under the bed—I also often encountered profoundly moving human dramas rife with intense emotions. Thus, I determined to write with both accuracy *and* intimacy in an effort to convey most honestly what these experiences mean to people. In addition, the ghosts encountered in this research did not always appear where I expected to find them, although they were often observed in unique kinds of peculiar spaces. That process of discovery proved to be as important as the content of what was discovered in the end. Thus, I determined to convey what was learned with both precision and aesthetic word craft within a unique organizational structure that allows the reader to make similar discoveries. To achieve these objectives, I took several creative risks, which occasions the following forewarning: expect an atypical book that is justified by an atypical topic.

ACKNOWLEDGMENTS

We are extremely grateful for the assistance we received in our research and in the production of this book. We particularly appreciate all of the people who met with us and shared their experiences of ghosts and hauntings. We also thank the Research Committee at Minnesota State University, Mankato; the scope and quality of this research was significantly improved by money granted via the 2013 Distinguished Faculty Scholar award. Numerous people provided enormously helpful assistance along the way. We especially thank Christopher Bader, Ally Beggs, Sara Cohen, Sarah Epplen, Simon Gottschalk, Janine Porter, Jeannie Thomas, Phillip Vannini, Dennis Waskul Sr., and Peggy Waskul. Finally, we are grateful for the patience and tolerance of our children, who uneasily endured our interest in ghosts, "family trips" to a graveyard, and frequent conversations about hauntings that they often found unnerving. We beg their forgiveness and apologize for any lost sleep.

GHOSTLY ENCOUNTERS

MINDING THE DEAD

On a cool evening in June 2013, I lie sleepless in my bed. Michele has been asleep next to me for quite a while, although I do not know how long. I have completely lost track of time. Frequently, and irritatingly, mind chatter keeps me awake, but tonight I am content with reflecting. Over the past several weeks, Michele and I have been intensely engaged in historical research and personal interviews mainly concerning one particular ghost. Like those in other stories we encountered in the two years that followed, this ghost is wrapped in drama and heartbreaking tragedy. This time I am fortunate to have discovered a plethora of historical documents, old photos, and descendants of the dead who are willing to talk to us. In a few days Michele and I will be visiting the location, said to be haunted, and on this night—my eyes peering emptily into the darkness of the ceiling above—I am organizing bits of information in my head, pulling up mental images of old photographs, shaping questions, and perplexing in the sadness of the story.

Our bedroom is essentially pitch-black at night. The television has been off for a long time; we have no nightlights or luminous clocks. A streetlight radiates behind and down the ally of our 1881 Victorian home, from which only a pale yellow light cuts through the bushes, trees, and fencing in the backyard—just enough to illuminate the window casing and immediate surrounding furniture inside. That's where I first saw it.

Out of the corner of my eye I see movement, and with my head still nested in the pillow I turn to look. In the top corner of the window, a pale, milky-white wisp is rising almost to our ten-foot ceiling—much like the gentle smoke from a small campfire, only lightly illuminated like fog before daybreak. I blink and wipe my eyes, to no avail. The wisp not only remains, but I can now see it coming through the window, through the blind, and gathering like a small cloud in the northwestern corner of the room. I am startled but not afraid. I am curious but prefer that it keep its distance. Mostly I am engrossed; I have never seen anything like this before (or since), and it fascinates me. My breathing becomes heavy and shallow and my skin tingles with a light electrical sensation as the pale cloud stems wispy tentacles that slowly reach out across the celling and down toward me. I do not feel threatened, but I distinctively perceive that whatever this is, it's intensely interested in me. A dozen or so wispy feelers beckon slowly closer.

I look over at Michele, still peacefully sleeping, and then back at the fascinating aura. I do not recall thinking anything at all at that moment. In fact, that is the most noteworthy part of the experience: a rare moment of absolutely nothing in my mind. If I had been think-ing, I might have been mindful enough to wake up Michele—it simply never occurred to me that maybe she should see this, too. Besides, the experience lasted no more than twelve to fifteen seconds, and the entire time I felt nothing but bewildered. Utter blankness in my head. Yet without any prompt or forethought, I calmly and softly utter two short sentences: "I will tell the truth. I will tell the story right." With that, the tentacles immediately retract as the wisp slowly descends from the ceiling and slips back through the window from whence it came—our bedroom, where I would remain sleepless for some time to come, once again encased in darkness.

I am not a religious or spiritual person; nor am I antagonistic to such beliefs. I'm just too preoccupied with the concrete and living pres-ent to devote much thought to a hypothetical afterlife, on the one hand. And on the other, I'm too pragmatic for existential dilemmas; religion and spirituality are just not useful for me, at least not now. So I do not have an answer for what happens after death or whether spirits of the dead can interact with the living, and most important, I do not need one. Like most people, I suppose, I have experienced things in life that I cannot explain, and I'm comfortable with not having answers. But I have never experienced anything like this.

I do not know what it was that I witnessed that night in June. Perhaps I was less sleepless than I thought and, having obsessed over thoughts of ghosts, my mind slipped into a partial dream state in which I witnessed a presence that was conjured by my own admittedly active imagination. I'm willing to admit that possibility. I am also willing to admit the possibility that I was, in fact, visited by an apparition that had its own reason and purpose. I don't find that difficult to accept, either. If you think about it enough, depending on definition, ghostly experiences are not necessarily all that unusual. After all, what is flat-ulence but the ghosts of the food that you ate?

I could choose one explanation or the other, but I won't. The pragmatist inside me knows better: the significance of what I saw that night is just as relevant either way. That is precisely why I told Michele what I saw and carefully documented the experience but have not otherwise spoken of it to anyone. This is my confession; here is where I acknowledge that cloudy wisp and give it due place. I understand that many, maybe the majority, who read my ghostly confession will dismissively say that it was all in my mind. Indeed—and it may come as some surprise that I mostly agree. But, wait. Allow me to explain before the naysayers don their satisfied smirks.

George Herbert Mead (1934: 50) articulated a profound understanding of the mind as that which "arises through communication by a conversation of gestures in a social process or context of experience—not communication through mind" and, for that reason, ceases to "seem mysterious or miraculous." He wrote, "Reflexiveness is the essential condition" of the mind (Mead 1934: 134). In short, mind is not something that we have; it is something we do—a verb. Therefore, minding appears in a multiplicity of forms: "thoughts, ideas, reasoning, foresight, imagination, understanding, judgment, deciding, choosing, evaluating, speculating," and more (Meltzer 2003: 253). That is why the ontology of what I witnessed that sleepless night is irrelevant. I minded it regardless, and necessarily "my experience is what I agree to attend to" (James 1905: 402). Thus, what I saw and experienced was not "in" my mind, because mind is not a tangible entity in and from which anything can "be." Instead, I reflexively minded what I witnessed—in thoughts, emotions, actions, and, ultimately, softly spoken words—and, to borrow from Mead again, it equally ceases to seem quite so "mysterious or miraculous."

It isn't hard to imagine how one would mind an unexpected encounter with something eerie, strange, or bizarre because we all do it. "The anomalous is a part of everyday life; people commonly have experiences that they cannot readily explain" (Thomas 2007a: 38). When something odd occurs, we either ignore or investigate. If we choose to investigate, most times we find an answer, and sometimes we do not, but either way we minded it. Oftentimes, if an answer is not found and the oddity is mundane enough, it is easy just to scratch your head and move on with your business. Once in a while it's not that simple. Now and then, whatever it was that you experienced may—or may not—have been a haunting, but it haunts nonetheless as you mind it in one way or another. Those are the experiences that fill the pages of this book.

Since the vast majority of the ghosts reported in this research said nothing directly to the living—that is, they did not speak per se—we listened to many accounts of people minding the dead. That is understandable. Consider, for example, the experience that I have confessed to you and the many ways in which I could mind it. After all, if such things exist in this world, then perhaps it makes sense that an apparition would be just as curious about me as I am about it—as if to take a look and ask, "Who is this sociologist and his wife? Why have they exerted so much time and energy to understanding ghostly experiences? And what do they want with me?" One must admit those are novel questions, perhaps especially for the living. Maybe the apparition really wasn't interested in me at all but came for its own entertainment, as if to say, with a sinister hiss, "So, you want to study ghosts, huh? Let's see what you do with me!" After all, it did turn out to be a test as I struggled with how to handle these "data," especially what I should say and to whom, how, and where. Or, perchance, whatever it was simply came to remind me of ethics: that I must speak the truth, tell the stories right, and do so in a manner that brings no harm to the living or the dead. In the years after, and the pages that follow, I have sought to keep that promise. As I said, I have not seen the cloudy wisp again, and while I would relish the opportunity, I take some comfort in the idea that maybe, because I have kept the vow I made that night in June, it no longer feels it is necessary to pay another eerie visit. Alas, there I go minding the dead once more, only now in a manner that explains what I no longer see.

Whether or not I saw a "real" ghost is far less interesting, or important, as the minded ways that I sought to account for it, the actions I have taken as a result, and the consequences of those actions. Those are the central dynamics that organize this book. And, yes, every night before I fall asleep I still peer at least once into that empty northwestern corner of our bedroom, only now with new eyes and a sense of wonder.

I

THE TROUBLE WITH GHOSTS

> The best evidence for the natural history of ghosts remains in the ordinary, the unconsidered, and the everyday.
>
> —ROGER CLARKE, *GHOSTS: A NATURAL HISTORY*

Our task in this book is to explore accounts of human encounters with ghosts, broadly defined. I recount many of the stories of ghostly encounters that were shared with us over the course of two years of data collection. Along the way, we will travel to places said to be haunted and, at times, delve deeply into historical records that pertain to eerie tales. This study has one main objective: to understand the persistence of uncanny experiences and beliefs in an age of reason, science, education, and technology and how those beliefs and experiences reflect and serve important social and cultural functions.

"I am sometimes asked what those who think they have seen ghosts have really seen," wrote Louis Jones (1959: 2) in his study of ghost stories in New York. "I cannot answer that with any great assurance." Neither can I. Certainly, the reported ghostly encounters that fill the pages of this book range from relatively mundane occurrences to highly dramatic and spectacular happenings. And, surely, all of us are quite capable of fashioning any number of rational twenty-first-century explanations for these kinds of strange accounts and hence brush off these so-called ghosts as hallucinations, fanciful interpretations of simple coincidence, products of peculiar psychological states of mind, or simply overactive imaginations. Skeptical cynicism is easy and not always, or even sometimes, without merit. Yet a snickering dismissal of ghostly encounters overlooks the obvious persistence of these experiences; how ghosts are, at the very least, kept alive by the telling and retelling of stories;[1] and how these ghosts are understood and function in everyday life. Our effort to understand requires that we suspend disbelief and frequently engage people as they struggle with their own doubts, and start with questions instead of answers. I invite our readers to do the same.

In the fall of 2013, I was speaking with an elderly man who expressed interest in our research. As with most of these kinds of conversations before and after, the man, who was tall and thin, had a white beard, and wore thick glasses, eagerly offered his own mysterious experience. He recounted in detail a time that he saw thirty-eight eagles soaring over Mankato, Minnesota, our mutual hometown, and his interpretation of that admittedly extraordinary sighting. I have heard many stories like his, and for good reason. At 10:00 A.M. on December 26, 1862, Brigadier-General H. H. Sibley carried out President Abraham Lincoln's orders to hang thirty-eight Dakota natives in Mankato. My hometown remains the site of the largest government-sanctioned mass execution in U.S. history, which is especially salient every fall during the Wacipi powwow that is held in honor of the thirty-eight executed natives. Their spirits are frequently seen in our hometown in a variety of forms even when the powwow is not under way. I listened to the old man's story with interest but did not reach for my pen, paper, digital recorder, or informed consent form.

On the surface there appear to be close affinities between, say, a person who sees an apparition hovering over his bed, a Native American who communicates with a dead ancestor, two college students who have a rudimentary conversation with a spirit on a Ouija board, and an evangelical Christian who has been taken by the spirit of the Holy Ghost. Or, as Tom Rice (2003: 96) similarly explains, "It is a small step to move from believing in the devil and angels to believing in ghosts." There are also important differences that make this

---

1. Diane Goldstein and her co-authors appropriately add that ghost "stories contain spirits; they capture them for us and keep them before our eyes, scaring us but containing that fright in narrative form" (Goldstein, Grider, and Thomas 2007: 4).

"small step" a much larger leap than it may seem. In fact, despite surface similarities, the devout Christian who attends church frequently, believes in faith healing and spiritual gifts brought forth from a
baptism with the Holy Spirit (including vocal gifts, or "speaking in
tongues"; prophecy; and miracles) is among the *least* likely to believe
in ghosts (see Bader, Mencken, and Baker 2010; Baker and Draper
2010) for reasons best articulated by David Hufford (1995: 18):

> The rationality and empirical grounding of belief are sepa-
> rate from its "truth"; many false beliefs are rationally held on
> empirical grounds (e.g., the belief that the sun went around
> the earth, as held in antiquity), and many true beliefs are held
> without rational or empirical grounds.

In addition, the various institutions that mediate between experiences and beliefs play a crucial role. Religion and spiritualism bestow
"core beliefs" (Hufford 1995: 29) that, to the faithful, can convention-
alize encounters with "spirits," just as the core beliefs of the fervent
empirical scientist may be inclined to dismiss them. Consider Christian demonology as one example.

The presence of demons in Christian theology is far from mysterious, as there are numerous references to demons throughout the Holy
Bible.[2] Their origin is readily accounted for: "The great dragon was
thrown down, that ancient serpent, who is called the Devil and Satan,
the deceiver of the whole world—he was thrown down to earth, and
his angels were thrown down with him" (Rev. 12.9). Henceforth,
these pure spirits—evil fallen angels—would breed with, multiply,
and maliciously afflict the living, including "Mary Magdalene, from
whom [Jesus] had cast out seven demons" (Mark 16.9). The Gospel of
Matthew is especially thick with references to those "who were possessed with demons," of which Jesus "cast out the spirits with a word"
(Matthew 8.16; see also Matthew 7.22, 8.28–32, 9.34, 10.8, 12.24–28).
Mark repeats some of the same tales, adding new details. One in particular stands out: the messiah commanded, "Come out of the man,
you unclean spirit!" And Jesus asked him, "What is your name?" The

---

2. In fact, at least according to Scripture, it is abundantly clear that Jesus spoke more
about hell than he did about heaven.

demon replied, "My name is Legion; for we are many" (Mark 5.8–9; see also Mark 1.34, 1.39, 3.15).[3] Since a Roman legion—the basic unit of the ancient Roman army—consisted of various cohorts of ranked and specialized divisions of soldiers (a total of 4,200–5,120, depending on the era of the Roman empire), the word "legion" implies not only hostility but also an enormously large population of evil spirits in a social organization of hell that, not surprisingly, is just as hierarchically ranked as the Catholic church itself.

Scriptures are rife with demons malevolently influencing the living: possessing people; tormenting them; causing insanity, blindness, muteness, and many other afflictions. Demons bring about both great strength and illness in addition to suicidal behavior, self-isolation, self-degradation, and violence. These biblical demons are terrifying, yet it is surely comforting to the faithful to repeatedly read that they are driven away and shown to be mere charlatans before the mighty power of God—although not to be trifled with nonetheless (see Acts 19.13–16). Since the Bible refers to demons with specific names and specific functions, the most frequent of which is Beelzebub (literally, the Lord of the Flies), subsequent Christian demonology conceives of these spirits as rank-ordered specialists of evil. Sitri, to cite one of many possible examples, is a prince of hell who rules over sixty legions of demons; he is a master of seduction whose evil specialty is to enflame people with lust and a desire to show themselves naked.

We have gone far enough into demonology to make the point: for the faithful, these kinds of complex and sophisticated belief systems can be understood only as a cosmology that conventionalizes the eerie while providing ready-made interpretive schemes for human activity in which ghostly spirits—demons, in this case—are always lurking about and therefore, perhaps, are not that uncanny in the end. After all, the demonic influence of Sitri, to return to our example, can be felt in everyday life inasmuch as it is observed in the

---

3. For Luke's accounts of demons, see Luke 4.33–35, 7.33, 8.27–33, 9.42, 11.14. It seems that John didn't have much to say on the topic, except for a smattering of accounts of how Jesus was sometimes thought to be a demon (see John 8.49, 10.21). Even strictly within the New Testament, this is in no way a complete list of the references made to demons, the majority of which contain the same explicit or implicit message: "if I drive out demons by the finger of God, then the kingdom of God has come to you" (Luke 11.20).

highly destructive, self-degrading recklessness of celebrities ranging from Tiger Woods, who apparently now has been excised of Sitri, to Anthony Weiner, the infamous political peter-tweeter.

The ghostly encounters that fill the pages of this book, unlike the awe-inspired story of visitations from native ancestors, baptisms with the Holy Spirit, and the casting out of demons with the Word of God, are experienced and understood *outside* powerful social structures and conventionalizing cultural beliefs. Certainly, some people in this study made use of their religious and spiritual beliefs to help interpret what they experienced or how they responded (e.g., by praying, burning sage, or calling a priest). However, for clarity it was necessary for this research to focus on ghostly experiences that lurk outside the nomos of religion and spirituality, which are equally worthy of study but fall into an entirely different set of social and cultural dynamics. In fact, it is the ghost who is neither conventionalized by religion and spiritualism nor explained away by science and reason that is the most potentially troublesome, partly because "such beliefs and experiences are dually rejected—not accepted by science *and* not typically associated with mainstream religion in the United States" (Bader, Mencken, and Baker 2010: 24).

THE TROUBLES THAT LURK

Ghosts are troublesome and in many ways beyond the obvious. Indeed, the obvious trouble with ghosts—their capacity to frighten and terrorize—is among the most misleading. Surely, the ghosts of popular culture are frequently horrifying, such as Freddy Kruger in Wes Craven's *Nightmare on Elm Street* franchise (1984–1991), who, out of vengeance against the parents who burned him alive, stalks and murders teenagers in their dreams. Likewise, Steven Spielberg's *Poltergeist* series (1982–1988) chronicles a family under attack from a league of ghosts controlled by a nineteenth-century religious zealot who is literally hell bent on abducting their daughter Carole Anne. Even comedies such as *Ghostbusters* (1984, 1989) portray ghosts as a terrifying menace who, in this case, would have destroyed New York City and beyond were it not for the awkward but well-equipped heroics of Bill Murray and Dan Aykroyd. Admittedly, these are popular films from my era of coming of age. Older readers will recall their own—perhaps *The*

House on Haunted Hill (1959), *13 Ghosts* (1960), *The Haunting* (1963), *The Exorcist* (1973), or *The Amityville Horror* (1979). Younger readers might recall *The Sixth Sense* (1999), *The Blair Witch Project* (1999), or *Scary Movie* (2000–2013). And surely, all of us can reflect on the ways that dastardly people evoked fears of ghosts (and other monsters) for selfish plots that were cleverly thwarted by Scooby-Doo (1969–present) and his motley gang of "meddlesome kids." In popular culture there is no shortage of terrifying and menacing ghosts.

Everyday ghosts are a different story altogether. From the earliest empirical studies of ghost lore (Jones 1944) to the more recent (Goldstein, Grider, and Thomas 2007), one conclusion is apparent: most often, ghosts of everyday life seldom do anything more than subtly make their presence known. Or, stated differently, given all of their otherworldly powers to defy the known laws of nature, the majority of everyday ghosts are dramaturgically impaired. Ghosts are most often indifferent to the living. When ghosts bother to pay us any attention at all, that attention is more frequently friendly and even helpful than malevolent. Indeed, as we illustrate later, the harm associated with ghosts is sometimes ironically the other way around: accounts of ghosts can bring harm to the dead, and occasionally it is the dead that ought to fear the living. Thus, Jones (1944: 246) concludes from his remarkable study of 460 items of ghost lore:

> It is assumed that a ghost will terrify. . . . The first observation must be that over half of the revenants are neither friendly nor unfriendly toward the living, but supremely indifferent to them. . . . These indifferent dead come for some minor purpose of their own and pay the living little or no heed. . . . They are neither sad nor glad, but preoccupied. . . . Almost never does a ghost hurt a person unknown to him, almost never does he act without cause. . . . Many ghosts come back in the best and kindliest frame of mind. They are helpful, consoling, rewarding, informative or penitent as we have already seen. Even, occasionally, they are in a lighthearted laughing mood, but these are rare. It should be reemphasized that the figures do not substantiate belief that ghosts need universally be feared. Those who have harmed the dead may well take care, but any-

one with a clear conscience is as safe with a ghost as with one of his neighbors.

Fifteen years later, in his extended analysis *Things That Go Bump in the Night*, Jones (1959: 17–18) more wittily makes the point again:

In all fairness ghosts have gotten an undeservedly bad name.
. . . [A] long-standing tradition has led people to think that meeting the dead is a harrowing experience and fraught with great dangers. This is nonsense and statistically unsound. What this country needs is a Society for the Prevention of the Defamation of the Returning Dead.

If, in contrast to the ghosts of Hollywood fiction, everyday ghosts are most often indifferent or benign, then on what grounds can they be deemed troublesome? Allow me to suggest a few.

The trouble with ghosts is they do not die. Of course, a ghost cannot die because presumably it is already dead or residing in some plane of deathless existence. Ghosts can be driven away, as with an exorcism or by use of a charm, but they are otherwise above death or beyond death. This is not, however, what I mean.

Scholars and academics of all kinds have confidently predicted that belief in ghosts, as well as all manner of the supernatural,[4] will fade into extinction with the scientific—if not evolutionary—

---

4. Throughout this book, I use the word "supernatural" sparingly and do not use the word "paranormal" except as part of the term "paranormal investigator." "Nature," of course, is an abstraction. Nonetheless, "nature" refers to a set of governing laws that can be observed, tested, and otherwise empirically verified. Thus, the "supernatural" is necessarily that which defies the known laws of "nature." We can accept this definition. More frustrating is the mismatched grab bag of what is deemed "supernatural": ghosts *and* aliens, Big Foot *and* extrasensory perception, demonic possession *and* déjà vu. Surely, there is an important difference between, say, the person who believes he was abducted by an alien and the person who believes she was comforted by the ghost of a dead mother in a time of grief. I am uncomfortable with the word "paranormal." At best, "normal" is a statistical abstraction. At worst, "normal" is among the most brutal(izing) concepts in the history of ideas. In contrast to "nature," there is no "normal" (except as an approximation); thus, in one sense of the word, all things are in some way paranormal.

advancement of society and culture.[5] The anthropologist Anthony Wallace, for example, confidently wrote that "belief in supernatural beings and in supernatural forces that affect nature without obeying nature's laws will erode and become only an interesting historical memory" (Wallace 1966: 264). "The process," Wallace adds, "is inevitable. . . . [A]s a cultural trait, belief in supernatural powers is doomed to die out, all over the world, as a result of the increasing adequacy and diffusion of scientific knowledge" (Wallace 1966: 265). The theologian Rudolf Bultmann expressed the same sentiment when he wrote, "Now that the forces and laws of nature have been discovered, we can no longer believe in *spirits, whether good or evil.* . . . [I]t is impossible to use electric light and the wireless and to avail ourselves of modern medical and surgical discoveries, and at the same time believe in the New Testament world of daemons and spirits" (Bultmann 1953: 4–5).

It is therefore not surprising that scholars have regarded belief in ghosts as idiotic or depraved—or, at the very least, in the words of the historian Keith Thomas (1971: ix), that ghosts have been "rightly disdained by intelligent persons." Newbell Puckett (1931: 9) stated it much more offensively when he deemed that folk beliefs of this kind "are found mainly with the uncultured and backward classes of society, white or coloured; and it is to such retarded classes rather than to either racial group as a whole that reference is made"—thus adding race and class antagonisms to this history of scholarly elitism. There is little doubt that "most academic theories have assumed that folk belief—especially beliefs about spirits—is false or at least unfounded, 'non-rational' and non-empirical'" (Hufford 1995: 11), or that "our whole civilization is so neurotically suspicious of anything remotely suggestive of the supernatural" (Wren-Lewis 1974: 41).

This brings us to a related trouble: *because a ghost seemingly defies rationality, the person who believes risks his or her credibility*

---

5. Scholars have also called the persistence of beliefs in the supernatural a dismal index of contemporary and backward ignorance. For example, Victor Stenger wrote in *Physics and Psychics* that he was "astonished that so many people in a modern nation like the United States still take the paranormal seriously" and that he "shudder[ed] at what this fact implies about the general state of scientific education in America" (Stenger 1990: 298).

and stigmatization. As Richard Kalish and David Reynolds (1973: 219–220) wrote:

> Knowing the skepticism that is attached to mystical experiences, many persons are reluctant to admit to such occurrences until they have ascertained that their listener is sympathetic. They know all too well the assumptions that persons experiencing the return of the dead are mentally ill, drug-addicted, or alcoholic, and they avoid exposing themselves to this attack. Even the possibility of risking laughter or teasing will undoubtedly be avoided.

Likewise, most contemporary scholarship on ghosts and beliefs in the supernatural hinges on assumptions of deprivation and marginality—that, in short, "unusual belief or experience must be more common in individuals who are socially marginal, deviant, or psychologically disturbed" (Emmons and Sobal 1981: 50). From this perspective, marginal groups of people—the poor, women, the elderly, the uneducated, racial and cultural minorities—are theorized as more likely to believe in the supernatural as a means to cope with the strains of their disadvantaged status in society (Fox 1992; Glock and Stark 1965). Related variants of this theory suggest that "paranormal beliefs arise in response to the alienation produced by crises of the human condition" (MacDonald 1994: 35), as well as by rapid social change (Greeley 1975; Lett 1992). In this view, the supernatural bestows a sense of meaning and control in the face of chaos and uncertainty. Scholars of this ilk tend to take either a religious or a secular approach to their conceptualizations of the alleged relationship between marginality and supernatural beliefs. Those on the religious side argue that salvation from existential crises is the comforting appeal of traditional religion, and accordingly, with a decline in religiosity people may be more persuaded by the supernatural as a substitute (Orenstein 2002). Indeed,

> religious narratives and experiences can offer similar experiences, but ghost legends come with fewer strings attached— one does not have to accept religious principles, participate

in an organized group, donate tithes, or even believe in order to feel the pleasant rush of possibility offered by a good ghost story. Supernatural legends invite their listeners into metaphysical mystery in a simple, come-as-you-are and do-it-yourself fashion. (Thomas 2007a: 46)

Those on the secular side argue that society itself has become an inescapably alienating "juggernaut," and supernatural beliefs are one pathway to an empowering, transcendental re-enchantment of everyday life—a view best expressed by Barbara Walker (1995: 5):

In mainstream American society (and perhaps in other societies, too), which prides itself on scientific advancement, technological know-how, educational superiority, and computerization of almost everything, the supernatural functions as a transcendental element. It goes beyond the mechanical, the empirical, the quantifiable, the provable, and beyond the immediate and practical. It resonates with the idea that even though we have advanced technologically, there still are elements and concerns that rest outside our arena of control or conscious understandings. . . . [I]t suggests an attempt to believe in and connect with a "larger" universe in a world that has become increasingly sophisticated and objective on the one hand and abysmally narrowed and single-focused on the other. . . . In such a world, where the individual may sense a certain loss of control, belief in the supernatural (itself quite possibly outside of our control) ironically returns more direct power to humans: We may feel powerless before the juggernaut of technology, but technology is powerless and perhaps irrelevant when juxtaposed with the supernatural—and beyond it all, humans still have access to their supernatural realms.

In this way, available scholarly literatures most frequently suggest, explicitly or implicitly, that there is something wrong with people or their social worlds—"whether conceptualized as marginality, deprivation, alienation, or deviance" (Emmons and Sobal 1981: 55)—that makes them compensate with absurd, albeit sometimes enchanting, superstitious beliefs (also see Friedlander 1995; Gilovich 1991; Kurtz 1991; Shermer 1997).

The persistence of these theories is perplexing, considering that they have little empirical support or merit. Rice found in his study, which involved 1,200 random-dialed telephone interviews with adults across the nation, "how poorly social background factors account for paranormal beliefs" and that "the deprivation theory is not especially useful in explaining who believes in classic paranormal phenomena. . . . People who are routinely marginalized, such as African Americans, the poor, and the less educated, are often no more likely than other people to believe" (Rice 2003: 101, 104). John Fox's study of General Social Survey data from 1984, 1988, and 1989 concludes that "reported paranormal experiences are largely independent of major sociodemographic variables and hence provide little support for cultural source explanations of reported paranormal experiences. . . . These findings suggest that deprivation theory has little empirical support" (Fox 1992: 429).

Indeed, and in contrast to the convictions that supernatural beliefs would vanish, Gallup polls for decades have shown that a *majority* of Americans—75 percent—believe in at least one of the supernatural phenomena surveyed (Gallup Organization 2005). In fact, Gallup polls clearly show that, over the past decade, there has been a significant *increase* in the number of people who believe in the supernatural, with demonic possession the only category showing a decline. Apparently, at the turn of the millennium, Satan was alone in his significantly decreased cultural capital.[6]

What differs is simply who believes in what. "The supernatural is democratic," as Jeannie Thomas (2007a: 46) writes. Ghosts are among the most common of the supernatural beliefs; in a random sample of 1,637 people, Christopher Bader and his associates found, "nearly half of Americans believe in ghosts" (Bader, Mencken, and Baker 2010: 44)—roughly the same number of people who believe that global warming is caused by human activity (see Leiserowitz

---

6. On the basis of a random sample of 1,648 Americans, Christopher Bader, F. Carson Mencken, and Joseph Baker (2010: 175) found that "the more education acquired, the less likely people are to believe in supernatural evil" and the "belief that Satan is the primary cause of evil in the world declines steadily and dramatically with income."

et al. 2012). Thirty-seven percent of Americans believe in haunted houses (Lyons 2005). Various studies indicate that women are more likely than men to believe in ghosts, hauntings, and witches (Bader, Mencken, and Baker 2010; Lyons 2005; Newport and Strausberg 2001), as well as in precognition and extrasensory perception (Fox 1992; Goode 2000; Tobacyk and Milford 1983), and that women are also more likely to report such experiences (Bourque 1969; Greeley 1975).[7] "More than a third of Americans believe that extraterrestrials exist, and another 12 percent are absolutely certain" (Bader, Mencken, and Baker 2010: 47). Men are more likely to believe in extraordinary life forms on the whole, such as Bigfoot, the Loch Ness Monster, and extraterrestrials and the UFOs in which they fly (Goode 2000; Tobacyk and Milford 1983).[8] Men are also more likely to believe in astrology (Lyons 2005). Forty-three percent of Americans "exhibit belief in ancient, advanced civilizations such as Atlantis," and "another 30% are undecided on the matter" (Bader, Mencken, and Baker 2010: 51). Common measures of social class (education and family income, in particular) "are not associated with the empirically supported measure of extrasensory perception, clairvoyance, contact with the dead, and mysticism"; neither is marital status (Fox 1992: 428). As this research also finds, with increased levels of education Americans are more likely to believe in haunted houses (Gallup Organization 2005). Some literatures report that African Americans are more likely to believe in classic supernatural phenomena (such as ghosts), while whites are more likely to believe in UFOs (Wuthnow 1978), although there appears to be no correlation between education and beliefs in extraterrestrials (Goode 2000). In fact, when it comes to education, Rice (2003) found that better-educated people are more likely to believe in extrasensory perception, psychic healing, and déjà vu—although the wealthiest and best

---

7. Some scholars have suggested that this "may also be due to a sexist association of women with nonrationality" (Emmons and Sobal 1981: 55).

8. "If there is a trend here, it appears that men are somewhat more interested in 'concrete' paranormal subjects. In theory, at least, it *would* be possible to capture, kill, or find concrete physical evidence for the existence of Bigfoot, lake monsters, or extraterrestrials—and men seem to enjoy the hunt. Women have greater interest in more ephemeral topics" (Bader, Mencken, and Baker 2010: 108).

educated may be the least likely to report beliefs in classic supernatural (Mencken, Bader, and Kim 2009).

And what about the religious people? Empirical data on the relationship between traditional religion and supernatural beliefs are much more complex and divided. On one hand, a negative hypothesis asserts that people who subscribe to traditional religious beliefs are less likely to believe in the supernatural, because it is an endorsement of spiritual beliefs that are outside of church doctrine. On the other hand, a positive hypothesis suggests that both traditional religion and the supernatural "affirm the existence of realities beyond the mundane existence of everyday life" (Wuthnow 1978: 71); therefore, belief in either one is more likely to be supportive of the other (Goode 2000). Various studies show that both of these hypotheses are true *and* false (MacDonald 1995, Mencken, Bader, and Kim 2009; Orenstein 2002; Sparks 2001).

As it turns out, there is a curvilinear relationship between religion and beliefs in the supernatural (Baker and Draper 2010), and the issue is best explained by the *structure* of those belief systems—not the content of the beliefs themselves (also see Bader, Mencken, and Baker 2010). "For those not strongly tied to a specific, exclusive religious tradition through frequent practice, there is a significant positive relationship between Christian beliefs and beliefs in the paranormal. Meanwhile, for those attending religious services frequently, the relationship is severely attenuated" (Baker and Draper 2010: 415; see also Orenstein 2002). Belief in ghosts (and the supernatural in general) is greatest at the mid-level of conventional religious belief and practice—that is, among people who have a nonexclusive spiritual outlook and are moderate in how they practice their religion, "in stark contrast to those whose style of belief is more absolute or certain, whether in favor of, or opposition to, conventional religiosity" (Baker and Draper 2010: 422; see also Mencken, Bader, and Kim 2009). In other words, the evangelical Christian and the radical empirical scientist share a bed when it comes to absolute and certain belief structures, and they are among the least likely to believe in things like ghosts. The rest of the moderately religious, or spiritually flexible, population—arguably, the majority—is more likely to believe.

So what are we to conclude? Clearly, belief in ghosts has proved just as impervious to extinction as ghosts themselves. Moreover, just as a ghost can be driven out of a person or place, the people who believe in ghosts are marginalized, despite evidence that those beliefs are *normative* among a large proportion of the population. Those who believe in ghosts are especially likely to be marginalized by scholars, for whom these kinds of unpalatable folk beliefs are, at worst, symptomatic of pathology and, at best, an amusing but otherwise inconsequential myth. In fact, the use of the word "myth" in the social sciences says it all: it is usually used to imply nonfactual, ignorant, and even patently false beliefs that aggravate the problems of society and the hardships people experience (e.g., "rape myths"). This is unfortunate, considering that a myth is traditionally defined as a sacred story—"sacred" because the stories concern morality, ideals, expectations, and cautionary advice and are important means by which people link the past with the present as they body forth into the future. Perhaps if we were to think of ghostly encounters and the stories we tell of them as various forms of myth and mythmaking, in the truest sense, we would not be so dismissive or shocked to discover that ghosts refuse to die or otherwise vanish from our private and public spaces.

The trouble with ghosts is they are cross-cultural and transhistorical, yet they must also be understood as a uniquely modern phenomenon. On one hand, various accounts of communicating or otherwise interacting with the dead can be found everywhere and throughout history. It can be argued that belief in and experiences with ghosts may be a historical and cultural universal: from ancient Egypt to the Aztecs, from the writings of Homer to the jinni of old Arabian religion. On the other hand, the whole of the supernatural is a decidedly modern innovation.

As Émile Durkheim (1915: 39) points out, the "supernatural" refers to "all sorts of things which surpass the limits of our knowledge; the supernatural is the world of the mysterious, of the unknowable, of the un-understandable." Hence, unto the supernatural we haphazardly assign an enormous range of sometimes overlapping and frequently contested phenomena: ghosts, demons, angels, witches, fairies, monsters, the occult, extrasensory perception, clairvoyance, telepathy, UFOs, alien encounters—indeed, everything (and anything) that cannot be explained by the accepted knowledge of our time. Or, at the very least, the "supernatural" refers to everything that we cannot *make* understandable through socially accepted means of knowledge production, especially, in our era, the application of science, reason, and technology. Hence, as Durkheim insightfully argues, the concept of the supernatural is necessarily a modern idea. There can be no "supernatural" without "the sentiment that a *natural order of things* exists, that is to say, that the phenomena of the universe [are] bound together by necessary relations, called laws" (Durkheim 1915: 41). He elaborates:

> When this principle has once been admitted, all that is contrary to these laws must necessarily appear to be outside of nature and, consequently, of reason; for what is natural in this sense of the word, is also rational, these necessary relations only expressing the manner in which things are logically related. But this idea of universal determinism is of recent origin. . . . [I]t is a conquest of the positive sciences. . . . In order to arrive at the idea of the supernatural, it is not enough, therefore, to be witness to unexpected events; *it is also necessary that these be conceived as impossible,* that is to say, irreconcilable with an order which, rightly or wrongly, appears to us to be implied in the nature of things. Now this idea of a necessary order has been constructed little by little by the positive sciences, and consequently the contrary notion could not have existed before them. (Durkheim 1915: 41–43, emphasis added)

Or, as David Hufford (1995: 24) similarly explains, "Telescopes and microscopes, computers and laboratories, years of training—all are necessary to make officially authoritative statements about the world. This reflects a shift in the construction of cultural authority that really crystalized at the end of the nineteenth century and beginning of the twentieth."

Thus, for example, Pliny the Younger (A.D. 61–115), a Roman letter writer, author, lawyer, and magistrate, wrote about what we would deem a classic haunted house in ancient Athens: in the night, one could hear the noise of clashing iron and rattling chains. The sound would come nearer and nearer until, suddenly, an apparition appeared: an old man, pale and emaciated, in chains. In Pliny's account, the terrors of this nocturnal apparition drove away living residents until the home finally was deemed damned and uninhabitable. When the philosopher Athenodorus came to Athens, he discovered the home, was impressed with its size and low price, and was not at all afraid of the ghost. When the noise and apparition appeared to Athenodorus, he did what apparently none of the other residents had thought of: he acknowledged the ghost, who then beckoned to him with one finger. Athenodorus followed the slow-moving ghost into the courtyard and carefully marked the spot where it suddenly vanished. The next day, Athenodorus had the spot dug, and the skeletal remains of a long-dead person entangled in chains was found. Once the bones were given a proper burial, the house in Athens was haunted no more.

The tale of Athenodorus's home contains all of the recognizable elements of ghost stories that we currently tell, some two thousand years later. There are, in fact, quite a variety of Greco-Roman ghost stories (see Collison-Morley 2009). That should not be surprising, since the ancient Romans believed in various shades of the dead for whom there were festivals, official days, and rituals by which the living and the dead routinely encountered one another. Because "anomalies are relative to the existing picture of what constitutes the normal" (Truzzi 1971: 638), the ghost, as we know it today, could not be conceived by those people or by any collective group of people who do not regard the universe as governed by immutable and empirical laws, no matter how much the stories resemble one another.

The trouble with ghosts is the many and varied ways in which they make themselves known to the living. Because a ghost can make itself known to the living in so many ways, enormously varied experiences end up lumped together more by convention than by what they have in common. My first cue to this trouble with ghosts appeared early in our fieldwork when I discovered that the word "ghost" often proved problematic. For many people, "ghost" implies a visual confirmation of some kind of evanescent form that is "perfectly recognizable but is unquestionably a ghost because of its translucent and somewhat film-like form" (Jones 1959: 11). For that reason, many participants in this study were not sure that they had encountered a ghost and remained uncertain that such phenomena were even possible, simply because they did not *see* something that approximated the conventional *image* of a "ghost." Instead, many of our respondents were simply convinced that they had experienced something uncanny—something inexplicable, extraordinary, mysterious, or eerie. They trusted what they experienced, knew they could not explain it in any rational kind of way, and were unsure about how to label it. Indeed, as Sigmund Freud (2003 [1919]: 125) observed, "The essential condition for the emergence of a sense of the uncanny is intellectual uncertainty," and experience often does not adhere to cultural constructions of a ghost.

This problem is exacerbated by the fact that a ghostly encounter can be experienced in "a wide variety of guises and forms" (Jones 1959: 5). Simply drawing from the accounts collected in this study—and the list is far from exhaustive—we can say the following:

Ghosts sometimes appear in a visual spectral form (most often as some kind of recognizable human appearance; at other times, as a spectral shadow, mist, or orb); sometimes as a disembodied voice (occasionally speech but more commonly audible human expressions associated with emotional states such as a moan, laughter, cry, or scream); and most frequently in no visual or identifiably human acoustic form at all.

Ghosts sometimes make an audible presence by what appears to be an invisible interaction with inanimate objects in the environment; "objects are heard but not seen" (Jones 1944: 244): they knock on doors, rattle windows, scratch on walls, make the distinctive sound of footsteps, and creak floors.

Ghosts sometimes manipulate inanimate objects in the environment: they inexplicably rearrange items on a shelf, hide things from the living, turn lights and other electrical devices on and off, leave gifts, open drawers, tilt pictures on walls, turn on water faucets, break dishes, and open and close kitchen cupboards.

Ghosts sometimes make a nonvisual somatic imprint on people: they make the living feel as if they are being touched or clothing is being tugged on; they bring about experiences of inexplicable cold spots, perceptions of being pushed, or choking sensations.

In short, unto the word "ghost" fall a huge variety of perceived encounters with "something," and the range of those somethings has little, if anything, in common except that the teller cannot rationally account for what he or she experienced. For our purposes, we also use the term "ghost" in this generic, catch-all form. However, in the course of our research, we discovered discrete kinds of ghosts that require distinction, because they concern particular kinds of experiences that have much in common: apparitions, phantasms, wraiths, poltergeists, specters, and phantoms (which we define and discuss in detail in Chapter 3).

As all of these various troubles indicate, ghosts are thick with social and cultural relevance. As the pages that follow illustrate, ghostly encounters, and especially the stories people tell about them, reflect deep-seated cultural beliefs. Not unlike sociologists, ghosts sometimes compel the living to harness their understanding of society, culture, and, especially, history to make sense of what they have experienced. As we heard from many people, ghosts embody our hopes just as much as our fears—at individual, local, and broadly shared levels. As many reported accounts show, ghosts challenge people to understand and in that way expose important everyday practices of both meaning making and "sense making" (Vannini, Waskul, and Gottschalk 2011). Ghosts articulate moral frameworks as they appear to us as spectral embodiments of good and evil, right and wrong, desirable and undesirable, and they comment on matters of human responsibility. And because ghosts continue to haunt our everyday lives, we summon the dead sociologically by uniquely examining how people report experiencing ghostly encounters.

Excellent bodies of literature are available on the ghost *stories* that people tell, particularly among folklorists (see, especially, Goldstein, Grider, and Thomas 2007). Excellent literature on *belief* in ghosts is also available, particularly among sociologists of religion (see, especially, Bader, Mencken, and Baker 2010). And there are excellent sources that describe the *history* of ghosts (see, especially, Clarke 2012). But, with the partial exception of Freud (2003 [1919]) and the much more relevant work of the folklorist Diane Goldstein (2007), no literature examines how people experience what they believe are ghostly presences and the consequences thereof. *Ghostly Encounters* seeks to change that.

ANTICIPATIONS OF THE UNEXPECTED

The content of this chapter is mostly the product of deskwork—the usual distanced academic labor that Richard Mitchell (2002: 49) aptly describes as "limited to an interview here or there, some week-end visits, and comforting review of mute books, articles, and news clippings." That changes with the chapters that follow, as we closely examine the ghostly encounters that people report and visit places with haunted histories. To ease this stark transition, I conclude with a brief overview of how the rest of this book is organized, focusing on the questions and key issues that each of the subsequent chapters addresses. Do not, however, expect any answers here—at least, not yet. After all, both the authors and the readers of a book about ghosts and hauntings ought to embrace the potential to be surprised by something unexpected. Anything less would be injustice to the topic. Along the way, do not be alarmed if you experience strange ambiances, for ghosts most certainly haunt the very pages of this volume.

Because the topic is innately interesting to most people, we enjoyed significant attention, as we conducted this study, from colleagues, the people we encountered daily throughout our research, and even our children, who at this point know far too much about ghosts than elementary-school students should. Not surprisingly, it is the stories that people told that elicited the most fascination, especially their dramatic content. To cite just a few, they include the ghost of a witch who haunts all those who step on her grave; the portal a woman showed us in her home that she believes is a gateway to the afterlife, around which she hears spirits and sees apparitions; and the shadowy specter with luminescent eyes that reportedly chased a young man and his friends out of a cemetery. The responses of friends, family members, and colleagues who heard these stories varied quite a bit; the most common response, however, was fascination, followed by skeptical rolling of the eyes, dismissive chuckles (or hisses of disbelief), and final punctuation consisting of statements or questions regarding the sanity (or sobriety) of the people to whom we talked. That response was not surprising, either, and most of the people we spoke to were all too aware of how their stories threaten their perceived sanity. In Chapter 2, "Ghostly Reason," we listen very carefully not so much to what people say but to how and why they say it. In so doing, we illustrate the complex relationships among rational thought, empirical observation, struggles with a will to (dis)believe, and what we can only superficially deem unreasonable conclusions.

In Chapter 3, "Ghostly Typology," we provide a highly descriptive classification that illustrates the rich diversity of ghostly encounters that were reported in this research. I distinguish among types of hauntings and forms of ghosts, identifying four types of hauntings (intelligent, residual, anniversary, and historical) and six major forms of ghostly encounters (apparitions, phantasms, wraiths, poltergeists, specters, and phantoms). Chapter 3 concludes with common characteristics of ghosts, regardless of form or type of haunting, and ends with rare accounts of truly terrifying experiences that are distinct from the normative ways people report experiencing ghostly encounters.

In Chapter 4, "Ghostly Legends," we take a detour and a road trip to explore such legends. It is a detour because, unlike in the previous chapters, those who recount ghostly legends often have not experienced anything eerie or uncanny at all. It is a road trip because, more so than in previous chapters, we developed Chapter 4's content through fieldwork—time on the proverbial road that branched out along many literal and figurative detours. Unlike the personal narratives that largely constitute the rest of this book, here we focus on stories that are told among various people over time—stories that are often richer and more dramatic. As is made evident, things do not have to be true to be consequential, and that which is "true" exists at many different levels of what is "real." In the end, even the skeptic will have to concede the reality of ghosts and their capacity to exert influence on the living and the dead.

The book concludes with Chapter 5, "Ghostly Speculations," in which I reflect on the two years we spent among ghosts and hauntings: the amusing and terrifying, comforting and tragic stories; the people met along the way; the time culling historical documents, carefully transcribing words and reflecting on photographs taken in cemeteries, attics, and basements. What general understandings can we distill from all of this? When people report a ghostly encounter, what, exactly, is it that they experience? What aspects of contemporary experiences with ghosts and hauntings merit further research? I conclude with ghostly speculations, for, in the end, all of these things haunt the margins of what can be reasonably concluded.

IF THE WALLS COULD TALK
(OR SING)

Martha meets with Michele and me on a cold, wet Sunday afternoon in October 2013. Considering her rich history of thirty-five years of various and persistent ghostly experiences in her home, we are eager to interview her. A former day-care provider and mother of three adult children, the stout, sixty-one-year-old woman wears a sweater and bifocals; she has salt-and-pepper hair and a warm smile. Martha is modest, comforting, and well organized, as attested by a typed sheet of basic notes she has prepared to help her stay focused and not forget important memories she wishes to share.

Over the course of an hour, Martha describes her ghostly encoun-ters, as well as those of her children and of visitors to her home. Many of these ghosts are disembodied voices that sometimes speak but most often simply are heard in the walls as a murmur of mumbled con-versations. Other incidents include sightings of various apparitions, along with the persistent pranks of at least one poltergeist that is espe-cially intent on hiding objects in her home. Considering the variety of extraordinary encounters over many years, Martha has concluded that within her home is a portal to the afterlife, and one room in particular hosts the greatest concentration of these extraordinary occurrences— precisely where she believes the spirits are drawn. When I ask to see the room, Martha generously agrees.

We stand up from the kitchen table where I leave my notepad and pen. Michele and I follow Martha through the living room of her 1949 home, into a narrow hallway, and take an immediate right into a small bedroom painted a dull yellow. As we walk in, Martha comments on how visitors to her home frequently report a feeling of peacefulness in the tiny bedroom. She asks me whether I can feel it. "Um, yes," I say, but only because Martha exudes a feeling of peaceful kindness to me. The room was once her daughter's bedroom and now has a few book-shelves, a television set in the corner, and an easy chair. Martha points to the corner of the room, above the television, where she believes the portal to be—a place where, as she explains, she and others hear a con-

gestion of "voices in the walls." Just as Martha says the word "walls," her arm still outstretched, she pauses and peers for a moment into the empty space. At precisely that instant, all three of us do, indeed, hear something.

We hear a voice reaching through the wall. It is the voice of man, but he is not speaking; he is singing. The voice is muffled and subdued. It takes a moment to recognize it, yet after a few brief moments we can hear the words sung rhythmically, "Who can it be now?" then the distinctive saxophone riff of the pop song with that title recorded in 1981 by the group Men at Work. Again we hear, "Who can it be now?" and the saxophone. Martha's face perks up; her eyelids lift as she turns to me with an astonished look that requires no words. Her expression voices the question that I know she is about to ask: "Do you hear that?" Before she can speak, I turn to Martha with a smirk and answer, "That's the ringtone on Michele's cell phone"—the cell phone Michele has left in her purse, in the kitchen, on the other side of that wall. All three of us explode into raucous laughter. That phone call, not from the dead but from Michele's mother, is impeccable in its dramatic timing, and the ringtone Michele chose could not have added more ironic humor to the situation or fit better with all that Martha has told us about situations in which she has wondered, "Who can it be now?"

It takes a while for the laughter to subside. The point, however, is that it is laughter in the first place—and we are laughing at ourselves for being duped momentarily by a well-timed, ironic, but nonetheless fickle coincidence. Martha finds it just as amusing because, after all, while she believes there is a portal to the afterlife in that room—and that its presence explains more than three decades of ghostly encounters in her home—Martha is definitely not crazy.

More than amusing, the entire situation is ironic. The voice that we heard in the wall came from a cell phone, another inanimate object—a contemporary "superartifact" (Ascher 1999; also see Goldstein, Grider, and Thomas 2007: 4–5)—through which disembodied voices can be heard. The parallels do not end there. The disembodied voices that we hear in our cell phones are sometimes known to us, and sometimes they are not. They are frequently human, but not always. They often call to us unexpectedly, and each time they have the potential to call forth different aspects of our selves; depending on the caller, we may feel required to be a parent, child, lover, employee, friend, or foe. They *bring to us knowledge, understanding, and messages from another place where we cannot be, because we can occupy only one physical space at a time. Michele and I live in a home with a security system that, among many things, sends a text message to our phones every time a door is unlocked—our house literally speaks to us through our cell phones. For at least the past century, there has been a convergence between ghosts and technology in general (see Clarke 2012: 273–285). Still, it is fitting that we heard a cell phone through that wall, and at that precise moment, considering that it's a profound technology of our contemporary everyday life that does what was once thought possible of only ghosts.*

2

GHOSTLY REASON

> Too often people assume that ghost stories are
> simple, trivial stories that are told by unintelligent,
> uneducated, "superstitious," pre-modern or
> antimodern "folk." ... [G]host lore must be
> taken seriously because it is serious—culturally
> meaningful, rational, and still very much a part of
> our modern and technological world.
>
> —Diane Goldstein, Sylvia Grider, and
> Jeannie Thomas, *Haunting Experiences*

When a person states, "I believe that I experienced a ghost,"
does it mean the same thing as "I believe in ghosts"? Is
belief *in* something the same as believing *that* something
happened or exists? These seem like absurd questions, since one statement appears to implicate the other, but ontology is not the same as
epistemology. Or, stated differently, what we take to be "real" is not
always the same as what we accept as valid knowledge or "truth" (and
vice versa). Peter Lamont (2013: 14) provides a helpful analogy: "people may believe that it is raining, or they may believe that it is not, but
nobody talks about belief in rain. 'Belief in' is reserved for things the
existence of which is somewhat dubious." Thus, for example, to believe
that witches exist is not the same as believing in witchcraft. Wiccan,
pagan, and neo-pagan witches undoubtedly exist, though "whether
they have any magical powers is, of course, another matter" (Lamont
2013: 15). "Believing in" is a usually a conceptual statement, whereas
"believing that" is an empirical one. There is—or, at least, can be—a
crucial difference between "believing that" and "believing in."

Beliefs are statements of conviction, opinion, faith, and confidence
in what is true or real, and they unavoidably hinge on a good deal of
trust. People "believe in" things that are not (or cannot be) subject

to rigorous empirical proof. That is why, as Lamont (2013) points out, nobody states his or her belief in rain—we can determine only whether or not it is raining—in contrast with, for example, believing in ghosts. But that's where Lamont's analogy ceases to be helpful.

Beliefs are less important than reasons. Reasons are the excuses and justifications we give ourselves and others about why we believe, regard things as real, and accept that which we call truth. Thus, the same empirical reason for why someone believes that contemporary witches exist may also justify why that person does not believe in witchcraft. Likewise, I can gather evidence and provide reasons for why I believe it will rain, as simply as someone who believes she or he has experienced a ghost can gather evidence and provide reasons to justify that belief. And what I take to be *real* may not prove to be *true* (the thunderstorm on the horizon may break up, change direction, or pass over without spitting a drop), just as the reasons my informant gave me may be true but not necessarily real (the evidence is convincing, but neither of us can be sure what it is or was).

To address these complicated issues, we focus on ghostly *reason*, and for twin purposes. First, "reason" is a noun, a basis or cause for some belief or action—as in a motivation or purpose—and we seek to understand the reasons that people claim to justify their ghostly beliefs. Second, and perhaps most important, "reason" is also a verb— to think through logically and to conclude or infer on sound judgment or good sense—and we seek to observe the processes by which people conclude that they have experienced a ghost. In short, we explore ghostly reason as both a noun and a verb: how do people conclude that they have experienced a ghostly presence and what motivates them to believe? Let's start with the latter: ghostly reason as a noun.

ARTFUL THEOLOGY AND CREATIVE SCIENCE

As a noun, "ghostly reason" serves as a motivation, and one that is perhaps most easily observed among participants in supernatural sub-cultures. Interest in and, especially, having had uncanny personal experiences compels some people to join supernatural subcultures, where they acquire specialized vocabularies, develop idioms, learn to gather and share evidence, and refine collective knowledge that sustains and develops their beliefs (see Bader, Mencken, and Baker 2010). Television programs such as *Ghost Hunters, Finding Bigfoot, Psychic Detectives,* and *Long Island Medium* may have aided in popularizing and, perhaps, somewhat destigmatizing these supernatural subcultures. Yet in stark contrast to the majority of Americans who believe in at least some aspects of the supernatural, only a small percentage of them appear to participate in or otherwise engage these subcultures. Unaided by the specialized knowledge and narratives of supernatural subcultures, then, how do people make sense of their ghostly encounters?

As indicated in the previous chapter, beliefs and experiences with ghosts "are dually rejected—not accepted by science *and* not typically associated with mainstream religion in the United States" (Bader, Mencken, and Baker 2010: 24). But this dual rejection occurs only at the level of the culturally sanctioned "official beliefs" (Hufford 1995) of institutions with the vested authority to credit or discredit individual beliefs and experiences. Institutionalized official beliefs are distinct from, and do not determine, how people appropriate knowledge and understandings in their own creative and artful ways. Institutionalized official beliefs, or what James Holstein and Jaber Gubrium (2000: 108) might call "cultural categories, which may be used as membership categorization devices," are "not invoked in any automatic fashion, but, instead, provide narrative resources for constructing each story" that people tell. Thus, I occasionally encountered people who had developed their own, unique ghostly cosmologies, and perhaps ironically, in each instance those people drew artfully from the very institutions that most directly discredit ghostly experiences: religion and science.

As Robert, age thirty-four, explained, "The Bible put forward plenty of groundwork for my belief in the supernatural." Robert drew from Revelation 12 (verses 7–9), in which Satan and his angels were defeated, "lost their place in heaven," and were "hurled to the earth." For Robert, those fallen angels were able to "make flesh and walk among us." Robert also appealed to Genesis 6 (verses 1–4), which he quoted verbatim, to further justify his conclusion: "the potential for otherwise spiritual entities to assume flesh" and, conversely, that "fallen angels can assume the spiritual form of the dead." He continued:

> Leviticus 17 is a chapter giving rules to the Israelites, and there
> are a number of verses in this passage that absolutely forbid

the consumption of blood, because "the life of all flesh is in the blood." I have taken that to mean that if something has no blood, it is not alive. Conversely, if something obtains blood, it can be made alive. If a spiritual entity were to drain a living creature of its blood . . . it is completely possible that it could become flesh.

Robert paraphrased Saul's interactions with the witch of Endor in the first book of Samuel (chap. 28). In his interpretation, Saul "found a woman who had a familiar spirit who was able to conjure up the spirit of the prophet Samuel. So this presents biblical evidence of the existence of not only what we would now call a medium, but of spirits that could manifest themselves." Robert added, "Another interesting passage is found in Ezekiel 1. It is a vision, but when you read the description of the chariot, it sounds very much like it could have been a type of UFO."

Robert had much more to add, but this brief overview is sufficient to illustrate his form of ghostly reason. Robert was among the few I encountered who professed a deep religious faith while also believing in ghosts (and other supernatural phenomena). Robert's faith in scriptures mitigated his ghostly reason while also providing him with resources to fashion creative theological narratives to structure his beliefs.

Aaron, age twenty-three, gave us a seemingly contrasting theory that he called the "Antarian connection."[1] He described it as "hypothetical connection human beings have that interlinks everyone to each other and the entirety of nature. This hypothetical connection is achieved through the frequency spectrum and the manipulation of lower frequencies via higher frequencies." Thus, for Aaron,

in theory, the explanation [for ghosts] could lie in a form of intelligent energy operating at the highest possible point of the frequency spectrum, and if said energy is in existence, it could permeate the universe and maintain equal control of each component part. This energy would operate at such high

1. The term "Antarian connection" may be inspired by the writings of the famous parapsychologist Barry Taff.

frequencies that it would slow its atoms to such a rate that time would be seemingly nonexistent. . . . It is simply the manipulation of lower frequencies, therefore making them visible. The question is: are we manipulating the higher frequencies to see them? Vice versa? Or is a universe-permeating energy controlling the whole shebang, which, again, in theory could explain why we perceive ghosts?

I suspect our readers are unable to follow the Antarian connection any more than we can, but that matters little to Aaron. And his more technical and scientific-sounding theory hinges no less on faith and creative appropriation of knowledge than Robert's theological account. Physicists are as unlikely to endorse Aaron's theory as theologians are to agree with Robert's interpretations of scriptures. But this also matters little to Robert and Aaron. What matters are the narratives they fashion, not endorsement, because "stories take shape on the occasions of their use, *as parts of the very identity projects for which they serve as resources*" (Holstein and Gubrium 2000: 116; emphasis added). In other words, what Robert and Aaron explained were not only their own, creative accounts for the existence of ghosts but also, and at least equally, narratives about *themselves*. The narratives Robert and Aaron shared were not intended to persuade an audience but were fashioned by, to, and for themselves—an "internal conversation" and an ongoing, open-ended creative project of fitting together what they accept as truth to explain that which is otherwise mysterious.

STRUGGLING WITH AND AGAINST
A WILL TO BELIEVE

> You hear these things, but when it actually happens to you it makes you reevaluate what you think and what you believe—what you think is possible. It opens your mind up to different possibilities that, just because it isn't black and white and right in front of you, doesn't mean that it's not possible.
>
> —LESLIE, AGE THIRTY-FIVE

Robert and Aaron are atypical—two of only four people we spoke to who offered any kind of even loosely assembled narrative to explain the existence of ghosts. Even those who were certain that ghosts exist and that they had personally experienced them rarely offered any justifying narrative other than a simple conviction that "the spirits of the dead can return to the living," as I heard repeatedly. These are people who openly confessed that they "believe in" ghosts and "believe that" they have witnessed them. Once again, "believing in" is not necessarily synonymous with "believing that." As we will soon see, it is far from unusual for people to believe that they experienced something that may very well have been a ghost but to remain uncertain or even skeptical that ghostly encounters are possible. Thus, the ghostly encounters of most people we spoke to compelled them not to create justifying narratives but, instead, to engage in a more urgent, immediate, and personal struggle with or against a will to believe.

Those who struggled with a will to believe openly confessed that they believed in ghosts and reported ghostly encounters that were most often affirming (sometimes entertaining) and frequently occurred within experiences ghosts help to facilitate. Riley, age twenty, for example, said that she was not a "church person" yet quickly added, "But I believe in spirits and ghosts." Having already learned that Riley believes she has lived with a ghost for the past two years, I said, "So tell me about the experiences you've had," to get the conversation started. She answered:

> Um [*long pause*]. Well [*longer pause*]. Our cat kinda does weird stuff. Um [*pause*], I know they say animals can see spirits and stuff. And there's times that the cat would run around the house crazy. And, um [*even longer pause*], I don't know. I'm trying to think [*pause*]. There's other weird things that have happened. Like in my room, the pictures of me and my sister in dance get moved. And I go to my mom, and I'm like, "Mom, why did you move my picture like that?" And she's, like, "No. I didn't even go into your room."

Riley continued this way for nearly twenty minutes, providing a slow, broken, and scattered account of bits and pieces of seemingly trivial and unrelated events. Sometimes Riley came home from school to find the television set in her bedroom turned on, but mostly she found random pennies and bobby pins in peculiar places in the home that she attributed to the ghost that she believed she was living with.

I was neither disappointed in the ostensibly superficial content of what Riley had to tell me nor frustrated by her strained efforts to put together a coherent, convincing account. Two years before our conversation, Riley's older sister, a high school senior at the time, had been badly injured in a car accident that put her into a coma and ultimately took her life. When it comes to her purported ghostly experiences, Riley said, "I don't tell people this stuff. I don't like to tell people." After an extremely long moment of silence, her eyes reddening as tears streamed down her cheek, Riley explained in a grief-laden voice, "I like to believe that it's her sending me messages. I don't want people to ruin that for me. That she is still here with me in some way. We were really close. It's comforting. Like, I know she is still there." In that moment, I saw an undeniable ghost in Riley's eyes, and one that materialized in her struggle with a will to believe for emotional reasons that were easy to understand.

Riley is not alone in her desperate struggle with a will to believe. Stacy, age twenty-two, was a bright undergraduate student. She was inquisitive and engaging, yet far from gregarious, speaking in a soft voice in an uncertain tone and frequently punctuating her words with nervous, self-deprecating sniggers. Stacy did not sustain eye contact for more than a few seconds and preferred to look away as she spoke. "I describe myself as an atheist but searching for something to believe," she said, her face tilted forward as if she were speaking to my desk. Her eyes briefly peered up at me from behind the jet-black hair with red highlights that partly covered her face. Over the next twenty-three minutes, Stacy explained several occurrences that she and her family had had with what they believe to be ghosts. Then came something I did not expect.

"A couple times, I attempted to summon a demon," Stacy said, "but nothing happened." Caught entirely off guard, I apparently looked a little staggered, and she quickly asked, "Is it OK to say this?" I reassured her that it was—that her words would be kept in strict confidence and that she didn't have to answer questions if she didn't want to. Stacy immediately responded, "No, it's OK. I'm just, well, it's just kinda weird." She continued:

I read online that [to summon a demon] you light candles and you do certain chanting while you draw the sigil of the demon you are trying to summon. Then you sign in blood, and the demon would appear. I did that for a couple different demons. Obviously, Lucifer. And then the demon Azazel. And then Belial.[2] I find demonology to be fascinating! So, I was like, I wanna talk to a demon! But nothing happened. I just thought it would be cool. But, yeah, nothing. No weird feelings or anything. Nothing. The first time I did this I was seventeen or eighteen and most recently when I was twenty-one.

"And these things don't scare you?" I asked. "No. They should, but they don't," Stacy replied. "I actually tried to sell my soul one time." *"Oh really?!"* I responded, this time showing bewilderment that, judging from Stacy's laughter, she found amusing. "So, how do you go about selling your soul?" I asked. With some nervous laughter, Stacy gave me the abridged version: "Oh, you know, the whole blood sacrifice thing again. Yeah, you're going to think I'm crazy now!" At the moment, I was certainly perplexed, but I did not think Stacy was crazy—especially after I asked, "What was the going price for your soul?" She paused for several moments, her eyes turned toward the ground. When she finally looked at me, her expression was serious as she bluntly stated:

In exchange for feeling better. I don't know if you have heard of it, but I have IBD, which is [*pause*] inflammatory bowel dis-

---

2. Azazel is a goat-like demon believed to have been among the original two hundred fallen angels (Baskin 1972) and responsible for teaching humankind how to make weapons and engage in warfare. Azazel is also Hebrew for "scapegoat," derived from a ritual described in Leviticus (16.7–10) that entails the release of a live goat into the desert "for making atonement." Belial is sometimes mentioned in versions of Deuteronomy 13.13 and Corinthians 6.15. Occasionally, "Belial" is used to designate Satan; at other times, it means "worthless people." When personified, Belial is believed to be a demon of lies, hostility, and corruption. Early demonology depicts Belial as once equal to Lucifer—a king of hell—or at least Beelzebub's equal. In the Book of Revelation, Belial is regarded as "the beast," and *The Dictionary of Satanism* describes him as "the most vicious of all the demons" (Baskin 1972: 57).

order. I get sick a lot: abdominal pain, nausea, and I was just like, "OK, let's try this." You know, instead of going to another doctor and getting more medications. . . . So I wanted to sell my soul to no longer have IBD, as well as depression, anxiety, and OCD. Just for some peace of mind. I know it seems really weird, but at the time it seemed to make a lot of sense. I was desperate.

Riley and Stacy wanted something, and they struggled with a will to believe as part of how they cope—in these examples, with grief and illness, respectively. Much more common, however, were those who struggled against a will to believe. They had experienced something inexplicably uncanny and openly acknowledged that it might have been a ghost, but they remained ambivalent and at least partially skeptical. Those who struggled against a will to believe commonly reported one of two reasons they reluctantly concluded that they had experienced a ghost. The first involved reports of uncanny experiences that occurred so often that previously ignored oddities demanded attention and consideration. These uncanny experiences were, in short, literally and metaphorically haunting. Dylan, age thirty-five, provided a good example:

I would watch TV downstairs [in the basement] and hear the front door very distinctly open. It was a heavy door and made a loud rubber squeak when it opened. And that damn thing would open. My mom put bells on the door, and those would rattle—the bells. Then I would hear "boom, boom, boom" up the stairs, down the hallway, into the new part of the house, and it would go into either my little brother's room or my room. Then that was it. And so [*pause*], I don't know. The first few times I just remember thinking, you know, "Whatever!" [*in a dismissive tone*]. But then this would happen, sometimes, in the span of an hour four or five times, which is weird. It wasn't just one time and done. It would go on and on, the same sequence constantly repeating.

These reoccurring uncanny experiences haunt Dylan because an isolated strange event is easy to ignore, but a habitually repeating one summons attention and commands consideration much more assertively.

The second involved reporting uncanny experiences that occurred in conjunction with other events that seemed too unlikely to dismiss as mere flukes. These, in short, are uncanny experiences that collide with what is deemed improbable coincidence. Consider, for example, Lee's experience:

> It was my twenty-first birthday, in November, and we decided we were not going to do anything for my birthday, so we stayed in. That night I was sleeping, and in the night there was this gush of really, really cold, frigid, icy air blowing in my face. And this is, like, in the middle of the night—and at the start of winter. We don't have any AC [air conditioning] on, we don't open the windows, and the heat is on. So it was kinda crazy to feel cold air in the room. I woke up and opened my eyes a little bit, just kind of peeked, and as soon as I did that, I got a slap across my face and heard a loud thump on the floor. I turned over and looked, and there was this girl with long hair wearing a white dress scurrying really quick toward the door. I blinked and she was gone. I mean, I live with all boys, and the room I was sleeping in was locked. There is no way anyone else could have gotten into my room. So that didn't make any sense to me at all.

Lee said he initially "didn't think much about it and went back to sleep," adding, "I figured I probably stayed up too late or something." A week later, the story took a dramatic turn:

> I went to the receptionist and told her we needed maintenance to repair our apartment door. She was typing away and asked for our apartment number. I told her, "My apartment number is 426." . . . [She] hesitated and looked at me and was like, "Does anything freaky ever happen in your room?" I kinda lied to her, like, "Umm, no. Nothing freaky ever happens in my room." And she was like, "Oh, OK, but just to let you know, a girl died in your apartment." And I was like, *What the fuck?! Like, wow!* And she said, "Yeah, she used to be my roommate."

. . . I asked the name of the girl that died in my room, and it was Janine Fox.[3]

Later that afternoon, Lee searched the Internet for the name. "I was reading some of the news articles that came out about [Janine Fox], and I wasn't really surprised by what had happened until I read that she died of alcohol poisoning on her twenty-first birthday," he said. "That's when it freaked me out, because she came and visited me on my twenty-first birthday." For Lee, the collision of unlikely coincidence was simply too overwhelming to brush off as mere happenstance. Perhaps Rebecca, age twenty-two, summarized Lee's experiences best when she said, "I don't really believe in ghosts, but sometimes everything comes together so perfectly that you just believe in it."

Every now and then, people reported experiences in which they simultaneously struggled with *and* against a will to believe. In other words, occasionally people wanted to believe while also remaining doubtful and skeptical. Rebecca also provided an excellent example of this. She moved from her native country to the United States at age twenty-one; shortly thereafter, her grandmother passed away. "The night she died was a really strange night," Rebecca recalled:

There was something always bumping against my window. And I was like, *Maybe it's rain.* I mean, I was alone in the house and didn't know what was going on. I got the courage to go out and look at what was going on. So I look out in the middle of the night, but there was nothing. No rain. Nothing. So I laid down back in bed and again something was knocking on my window. This went on for hours. The next morning, my dad called and said that my grandma had died. And in my head, I was like, *What if that was her and she just came to say goodbye to me?* I *wanted* to believe that, I think. It never happened before, like something weird knocking on my window for hours—and there was no tree, no rain, and I looked *everywhere*.

---

3. Janine Fox is a pseudonym.

"I'm not a believer," Rebecca flatly stated almost immediately after she told the story. Yet eleven words later, she paradoxically repeated, "I want to believe," and proceeded to reveal a bit more. Rebecca had lost her last remaining grandparent that evening. "I felt guilty that I moved here," she said. "I didn't spend much time with her. . . . I was always busy and didn't go to visit her often." Hence, as Rebecca stated for a third time, "That is why I want to believe that I had a connection with her before she died." Rebecca then turned her face away from me, stared into an imaginary distance for a while, then slowly and softly concluded, "As if she came like a ghost to me, or she watched over me, and she knew . . ." *Knew what?* I wondered as I waited patiently for Rebecca's next word. But my unasked question would not be answered. There was only silence as she raised her right hand to her swelling eyes.

After several moments of silence, I asked Rebecca why she was so reluctant to believe. "Because it's not proven," she barked. With no trace of the previous emotion in her face, she began speaking rapidly:

It's hard for me to believe in something that there is no proof of. I mean, when you are a child, everyone believes, and you believe in miracles and stuff—you believe more in things. But when you grow up and you never actually saw a ghost—I mean, if I had seen, I'd be, like, "Oh my God! It actually exists!" But I never saw it. I just heard something, and it could be anything.

Finally, Rebecca conceded in a much slower and softer voice, "But who knows? I think about it sometimes. *I think about her,* but I don't know what to believe" (emphasis added).

Rebecca may not know what to believe, but the emotions of those few moments were intense and quite real—just as real as her longing for a deeper relationship with someone, a connection she now recognizes as a lost opportunity. Whether she believes or not may be less relevant than the morality implied in her telling of the tale—the life lesson that Rebecca seems to have gleaned from it—or simply that the strange occurrences of that night compelled her to remember a loved one, albeit with some guilt. Rebecca struggled with and against a will to believe not only because of an inexplicable eerie knock on her window one sleepless night but also perhaps because that experience evoked powerful emotions that she knew all too well.

A SUCCESSION OF DOUBT

> Having some time to process all of this, I just [*pause*], I don't know. I just think it's comforting to know that if I see or hear things, I'm not losing my mind. Like it's actually, or at least possibly, there. I mean, who knows what's real and what's not? But at least now I have a reason for it—like a rational reason for me personally.
> —KIMBERLY, AGE TWENTY-TWO

Struggles with and against a will to believe illustrate the complexity of ghostly encounters and how the meaning of these uncanny events ultimately is highly situated, contingent, and emergent within a context of interpretation over time and sometimes in ways that are both intensely personal and emotional. Indeed, the ghost is seldom self-evident and is rarely a static event that people passively observe. In fact, ghostly encounters are not an event at all. They are the result of a *process*. Reflect for a moment on the ghostly experiences that have already been shared. Pay attention to how people reported the uncanny events. In nearly all instances, it wasn't called a ghost until something *else* happened. The strange taps on Rebecca's window one restless night had no particular significance until she received the phone call from her father the next morning; Lee had already dismissed his encounter with the apparition on his twenty-first birthday and probably wouldn't have given it a second thought, if he had not later learned about the tragic death of a former resident of his bedroom.

The process by which uncanny events become ghosts is a highly individualized and contextual process of actualization. Riley's ghostly encounters, for example, obviously have to be understood in the context of grief and a desperate longing to have her sister's continued presence in her life. Yet each person I spoke to told of ghostly experiences that, in their own ways, were unique to a particular individual; to a small, tight-knit group (usually family or friends); or to the history of a specific place. Indeed, ghostly encounters quite often are so endearing precisely because they deeply relate to the biography of an individual, his or her immediate networks of others, and the physical world in which lives are lived.

Despite their highly individualized and contextual nature, uncanny events become ghosts out of at least one common process that is all about contending with doubt. When people experience something uncanny, they seldom immediately conclude that they have experienced a ghostly presence. Instead, strange happenings become ghostly encounters most often in a patterned process by which people contend with three successive layers of doubt: self-doubt, a doubting of what is real, and, finally, a doubting of what is true.

The first layer, *self-doubt*, is an immediate distrust, denial, or dismissal of what has been seen, heard, felt, or otherwise experienced. For example, in a previous illustration, Lee was awakened at night by an apparition that he both saw and felt, and his immediate reaction was to discredit it: "I didn't think much about it and went back to sleep. I figured I probably stayed up too late or something." People commonly report this same kind of self-doubt as the immediate response to uncanny experiences:

> It happened before, but I just brushed it off—or thought somebody was just messing with me. (Tara, age twenty-seven)

> I thought it was just my eyes playing tricks on me. (Aaron, age twenty-three)

> So, yeah, I thought it must have been the wind or something. (Nikki, age eighteen)

> It kinda freaked me out for a second. But I thought I've been kinda stressed out, and I'm tired, and blah, blah, blah. (Dylan, age thirty-five)

Unless it is forgotten or ignored, self-doubt remains in most instances until the uncanny events occur frequently enough to be acknowledged as more than a delusion or a strange but nonetheless isolated and insignificant event:

I try blaming it on my cats, but I don't know how my cats can get into my cabinets. Maybe I'm not perceptive, and I just don't really believe in ghosts and shit, but I don't know how the fuck this stuff keeps happening. (Tara, age twenty-seven)

Every few nights my radio would turn on at a certain time in the night, and I'd have to crawl off my bunk bed to turn it off—and it would always be the same song: *Candyman* by Aqua. Always that same song, and I'd have to crawl down [from my bunk bed] in the dark to turn it off. . . . [T]hose kinds of things happen so often. Unless I'm crazy [*laughing*]. But it happens a lot. (Maggie, age twenty)

For the first couple weeks, I thought, *Oh, I think I saw something, but it's no big deal. Whatever.* I didn't really think about it. But then it got to be too frequent—to the point where I noticed it more and started to wonder why I keep seeing something. (Paige, age twenty-five)

In contrast, self-doubt in other instances disappears the moment uncanny events are witnessed and confirmed by someone else. I say more about the credibility of multiple witnesses soon, but for now Aaron stated it sufficiently well when he explained, "For a little bit, I thought maybe I was just hallucinating. Or maybe I was going batshit crazy. But the thing is, people other than me started to see them. I mean, my friend Jason actually said, 'There is something standing next to you!'"

"Once the possibilities of human hoax, disordered senses, and misinterpretation of sense-data are eliminated," writes Erika Brady (1995: 147), "the exceptional remains, begging interpretation" as people seek out answers. Thus, once self-doubt is adequately resolved, the second layer of the succession is to *doubt what is real*: a highly rational, systematic, and empirical investigation that is "less about convincing an audience that the events took place and more about the narrator explaining how it was that he or she came to understand what happened, how it happened, and why it happened" (Goldstein 2007: 78). By way of example, let us begin with a curious home that houses restless objects.

In a midsize town—call it Midwestern, USA—there is a 1914 Craftsman-style home where inside objects move on their own. Objects both large and small sometimes move slowly over time, while at other moments they travel quite dramatically—such as a ball rolling across the floor, as if lightly pushed by an unseen hand. Unlike most of the events reported in this study, Michele and I witnessed these objects ourselves and are certain that the phenomenon is real. Yet the homeowner does not believe the house is haunted, and the movement of the objects is no mystery at all. It is not a ghostly force that is pushing the objects. Rather, it is a law of physics that is pulling them.

The house is handsome and well preserved, with much of its external and internal character in beautiful original condition. But even the most steadfast stewards of historic preservation cannot thwart all the ravages of time. For over a century the home sat where it was built, and the foundation has settled unevenly. That is not uncommon for a home that is over one hundred years old. The western side of the home has sunk considerably lower. We placed a laser level on the floor against the interior eastern wall, and on the opposite wall the bright red beam dramatically reveals that the house is approximately two inches lower to the west. Of course, objects inside this house will seem to move on their own—especially round objects on the hardwood floor.

Throughout the pages of this book are repeated references to places of antiquity, and especially old homes. Surely, there are some who may mistake the qualities of an old home for a ghostly presence—such as a ball rolling across the floor because of unevenness in how the house has settled. But there is more. That same unevenness also ensures that the rooms inside the house are seldom square, and that can result in a visual perception that something is strangely "off" (because something is). Old homes also articulate: floors squeak, stairs groan, hinges whine, window panes clatter, changing temperature in the plumbing causes crackling noises in the walls and floors, and fluctuating water pressure can create a "water hammer" in the pipes that emits vibrations and sometimes makes a surprisingly loud rumble or boom. Old houses often breathe freely: enough to create sudden changes in air temperature and make curtains move and doors rattle nervously on a breezy day. Over time, non-human animals may take residence in unoccupied spaces of the house—hornets, rats, mice, squirrels, and various other varmints that make an assortment of peculiar sounds. I grew up in an 1871 Italianate Victorian home and was sometimes awakened at night by the pattering sound of the many bats that fled into and out of the chimney behind a wall adjacent to my bed—and knowing they were bats, not ghosts, was not necessarily comforting, I must add.

It is likely that some people mistake the qualities of an old home for a ghostly presence, but we found no evidence of that among the people we spoke to. In fact, we found quite the contrary. The people we spoke to were almost universally "rational believers" (Goldstein 2007: 66): not easily duped, aware of these and other aspects of their physical environment that can be mistaken for an uncanny experience, and willing to posit a ghostly presence only after systematically eliminating these and other sensible explanations. As Dylan said, "I have always used science or a very clear-cut explanation on anything paranormal to explain things before I could believe it. Either I need to see it firsthand or need credible scientific proof of its existence."

"Scientific proof" of the existence of ghosts is highly unlikely, although paranormal investigators may disagree or perhaps succeed in that objective one day. Nonetheless, in the process of doubting what is real, people routinely rely on an approximated scientific method to make empirical observations, formulate inferences, identify correlations, arrive at working hypotheses, and sometimes even test those hypotheses. Consider, for example, the process by which Amy, age nineteen, determined that she is living with a ghost. Amy lives with a poltergeist she affectionately calls "Frank." Like most poltergeists, Frank is a noisy roommate: "cabinets banging, footsteps—lots of footsteps—I'll think my roommate is home and she's not. So, I mean, just those kinds of occurrences," Amy said nonchalantly. Frank is also typical of poltergeists in that he hides and rearranges things in Amy's apartment and is especially drawn to a small plaque placed prominently on Amy's television stand that reads "Live one day at a time" (Amy's sister gave her the plaque when she was hospitalized a few years earlier). "There's no windows near this plaque; there's nothing that would make it move," Amy commented. "Sometimes Frank shifts it over just a little bit, but not enough to make it significant." At other times "the plaque is literally turned completely facing my bedroom. And no one was home." These things bother Amy quite a bit. "I'm a little OCD with things, and the plaque is always straight," she said. "It *needs* to be straight. Otherwise, it drives me nuts."

When I asked Amy, "What convinced you that you're living with a ghost?" she replied, "Because of all my tests I do with him," and provided an example: "One day, I told Frank to move the plaque. I told him, 'When I return to the apartment, move the plaque so that it is facing my bedroom door.' No one was home. I left with my boyfriend and locked the apartment door." When Amy returned from her date, she said, "I sat down on the couch, covered my mouth, and was, like, 'No way! I can't believe that happened!' The plaque was directly facing my room." Amy further added:

I don't automatically jump to "Oh, it's a ghost!" . . . I try to debunk it in some kind of way, shape, or form. I literally jumped right next to our TV to see if the plaque would shift. I checked to see if the windows were open. It was all the unexplained stuff and me testing him. Asking him to move the plaque is the obvious one. I mean, he would move it a little, little, little, but not anything dramatic. So I physically showed him to turn it the way that I wanted him to, and he did it.

Amy's tests would not pass "a double-blind test in laboratory conditions" (Bader, Mencken, and Baker 2010: 37), but they work for *her*, and above all, they are far from irrational. In fact, Amy is clearly engaging in an approximation of the scientific method. In scientific terms, Amy's tests allow her to confidently "reject the null hypothesis"—the most central of all practices in modern science and precisely that which is necessary to conclude scientifically that there is a relationship between two phenomena—and it's enough to satisfy Amy's doubts about what is real. In cases like Amy's, "the tests were not exhaustive, to be sure, and they were not performed in a rigorous fashion, with independent variables held constant and a single dependent variable tested, but the lack of scientific expertise does not belie the presence of scientific intent" (Pimple 1995: 83).

Amy eagerly showed me a photograph she took of one test she conducted to determine whether Frank is real, commenting, "I'm glad I finally have proof of it"—a sentiment I encountered many times. Often in the course of this research, people enthusiastically showed, and usually gave us, photographs of mists, orbs, inexplicable hand prints, and other oddities.[4] I received one video, taken with a "nanny cam," that captures a bright wisp moving quickly behind a couch. There the wisp briefly pauses, and one can see a child's face materialize in the haze at about three feet in the air. Then, suddenly, the wisp darts into the kitchen and disappears. The current owners purchased the home from a couple whose young child died choking on a grape. Tara, age twenty-seven, lives in a home where a poltergeist dramatically tilts her grandmother's artwork that hangs on the walls—she shared photographs of herself and a friend that were taken before a girls' night on the town. "Look in the background," Tara said as she flipped through the several images on her phone: successive silly photos of her and her friend in which the large framed artwork

---

4. Most people gave us permission to reprint those images in this book. Unfortunately, in all instances the images were taken with smartphones and could not be reproduced at a resolution high enough to be useful.

in the background vividly moved from horizontal to tilted a good three inches to the right.

The regarding of photographs and videos as significant evidence is understandable. In the process of doubting what is real, not all evidence is of equal weight. In an era in which "seeing is believing" and in a culture in which "sight is supreme" (Synnott 1993: 206), visual evidence is regarded as the most robust means to determine what is real:

> I've already seen things being moved around—so I'm pretty sure something is there. (Tara, age twenty-seven)

> I can't just say, "Oh, that's just bullshit." I mean, I can't just say that about things that I've seen personally. (Josh, age twenty-three)

> I like to see to know that it is real. (Gwen, age eighteen)

> I mean, you can't chalk it up as coincidental if I saw that before he had said anything. (Vicki, age nineteen)

> That was pretty far-fetched for me, but I also don't doubt my eyes, either. (Amy, age nineteen)

The most robust of all evidence is not just visual confirmation but visual confirmation by multiple witnesses—not unlike what statisticians call "inter-rater reliability," a highly useful procedure used to determine whether a measure is reliable. In short, when two or more people consistently produce the same findings, one can be confident that the measure is reliable (although not necessarily valid). Once more, people approximate this scientific principle as they contend with their doubts about what is real. For example, Henry, age forty-nine, who lived in a farmhouse built in the 1930s, said:

> The house was an amazing structure, and it always had a certain presence to it. We had a first contact with an actual visible presence—a manifestation of what we were feeling there. We saw the aura, or more of an outline than anything. It was a

woman and two children. . . . My wife and I would sometimes
wake up in the middle of the night and have the sense of their
presence in our bedroom just kind of watching us. It was never
alarming. It was just an interesting part of living in that house.
It was always the same three people together—the mother and
two children. We would see them maybe once a month or so
over the period of two years that we lived in the house—so
very frequent! It was always at night. We would just wake up
for whatever reason and they would be there. . . . I felt certain
that it was a ghost when we had watched them for a period of
minutes and both of us [were] just kind of lying there, looking
at each other, then looking back and it still being there. [We
were] actually, looking down the foot of our bed at the apparition and back at one another, like, "Are you seeing this?" . . .
That's when we were sure we were not just sleeping. If it were
just me seeing this, yeah, I probably would have thought I was
just hallucinating and rolled over and gone back to sleep.

The *credibility* of additional witnesses is also frequently cited in
the process by which people contend with doubts over what is real.
Especially significant are former skeptics and the innocent. When
professed nonbelievers concede and confess to experiencing uncanny
events, people frequently report feeling much more confident that
what they are experiencing is real:

My dad is such a skeptic on everything. So when he started
telling me things. . . . That's when I started thinking something real was going on. (Dylan, age thirty-five)

My boyfriend is a huge skeptic, and for him to see those two
incidents for himself [was], I think, a huge slap in the face.
(Amy, age nineteen)

One night when my sister and her husband were staying overnight—and it gets cold in here; it always has—my sister said it
got really cold, so she went to get more blankets. Her husband
woke up when she left the bed, and he really doesn't believe

in this stuff, but he saw a lady rocking in a rocking chair. He thought, *Nooooo*, and went to get his wife, and it disappeared. (Martha, age sixty-one)

My parents never believed me until they saw something themselves. (Maggie, age twenty)

The innocent are also frequently cited as credible witnesses, mainly because people perceive their actions and accounts as untainted by ulterior motives, especially if they are unlikely to have prior information about the possibility of a ghostly presence. For this reason, when children spontaneously report ghostly experiences that corroborate what adults are experiencing, the adults often report feeling confident that what they are experiencing is real. Nora, age forty-three, for example, lives in a home with her husband and elderly father in-law. She is certain the house is haunted, but it has taken her years to arrive at that conclusion. Shortly after moving into the house, Nora said, her husband and father in-law

sensed a presence and felt that they were never really alone in the house. My husband one evening was in the living room watching TV and saw movement. He watched what he described as a black shadow move through the living room, down the hallway, and to the bedroom at the end. My immediate response, at that point, was, "You watch too many scary movies. You're seeing things. We don't have any kind of spirits or ghosts in our house, and don't tell me about it."

Nora and her husband continued to experience inexplicable happenings in the house, but she also stubbornly refused to attribute any of them to a ghost. But all of that would change one night when a child who had no prior knowledge of the purported events occurring in the home corroborated what they were experiencing. As Nora recounted:

We had a friend's eight-year-old son staying at our house overnight. When it was bedtime, in the last bedroom at the end of our hallway, he was sleeping on the bottom bunk. That night he sat up and was looking at something and was, like, "Cool!" He climbed to the top bunk where my daughter was sleeping, and she was, like, "What's going on? What are you doing?" And he said, "Don't you see it? It's a ghost!" . . . So that was when I just accepted there is a ghost in our house.

Nora offered additional evidence: "We had a dog at that point, and he looked up at the same time that my husband noticed something. We noticed the dog was also watching." Nora was not alone in trusting the credibility of non-human animals. Leslie, age thirty-eight, explained:

We got a cat—and her name was Molly—and she started to do some strange things, and that's when we started noticing strange things. The lights would flicker at night, or the pots and pans would rattle in the kitchen. When those things would happen, I remember [Molly] going up on top of the couch in the living room—where we were—and she would sit up on the couch, and she would peer her head around the wall that was dividing the living room and dining room. Her hair would raise up; she would growl, looking toward the kitchen. She would not go toward the kitchen, and was really upset and touchy.

Like the children perceived as innocent, non-human animals that responded to apparent ghostly presences were regarded as credible witness:

One night the dog kept barking at that chest over there [*pointing at a 1930s buffet in the dining area*]. [She was] up on her hind legs—like, "pick me up"—barking at something. Then she would walk away, and then come back and bark at it again. She has not done that since and hadn't done it before. We were laughing so hard, because, like, "What are you barking at?" We tried moving things. What was she seeing? Was she seeing herself? I think she was seeing somebody. (Martha, age sixty-one)

I never *saw* anything, but we had dogs—and the dogs would see things. . . . [S]o, like I say, I felt and heard this presence behind me but nothing was there. And I look across the room, probably about twenty-five feet, and my dog was in the doorway. She wouldn't come in the room and was all freaked out. Her hair was up, and [she was] making this, like, whimpering sound—like, "I'm worried about you"—but she would not come to me. I looked at her and thought, "Oh my gosh!" It definitely creeped me out. I mean, I didn't feel like it was evil or anything, but that definitely made me feel that something else was in the house. (Jackie, age thirty-eight)

It was just this uncomfortable feeling of something, and my pets sense something, and it was uncomfortable. I mean, why would my animals be freaking out if there truly was nothing there? (Kimberly, age twenty-two)

Once people have adequately resolved their doubts over what is real, the last layer in the succession is to *doubt what is true*. At this layer in the succession, people express certainty that they have experienced something uncanny but question the cause or source of those strange occurrences. Some, like many of the informants already cited, conceded that they had a ghost in the house and, in their own ways, confess to having overcome their doubt (e.g., "I have no doubt in my mind," as Dylan, age thirty-five said, or "I feel like they do exist, as much as I don't want to admit it," as Bell, age twenty-one, said). But not everyone was so certain. And certainty that something uncanny has happened is one thing; attributing inexplicable occurrences to a ghost is something else altogether. Thus, some had no doubt that the uncanny events they experienced were real, yet they continued to express misgivings about their truth:

I've analyzed it, and thought about it, but all the experiences that have happened are so different from one another and have happened to different people. I dunno. None of the times are consistent. It's always random. And I can't make sense of it. (Diane, age twenty)

So, um, essentially I'm not ruling out the possibility of that being possible. I mean, there is so much about the world that we really don't know. Yeah, part of me wants to chalk it up to coincidence for some of the stuff, and part of me is a believer. So I just can't rule it out. It's always one of those things in the back of my mind where it's like, "Yeah, it could be." After years of reasoning with it, I have to say that I believe that it is possible. I mean, whether it's what we know as a spirit, or whether it's another plane of being—who knows. (Josh, age twenty-three)

Uncanny events become ghostly encounters in a complex process. While it is true that those who report beliefs in and experiences with ghosts "are often perceived as a little bit 'nutty,' if not completely crazy" (Bader, Mencken, and Baker 2010: 7), the more closely we look at the reasons people hold these beliefs and, especially, the empirical, systematic, deductive process by which they arrive at the beliefs, the less "nutty" or "crazy" they appear—usually, at least. There are some people who cling to non-normative views of this world and beyond—such as Robert and Aaron, cited earlier—but they are the exception. For everyone else, the ghostly encounters they report are "reasoned and logical" because the stories they tell "appear to be largely about reasoning and logic" (Goldstein 2007: 71). But there is more, and something that I hope readers have been able to discover for themselves by now.

Ghostly encounters are often and equally about profound human dramas that are sometimes laced with intense emotions—grief, despair, desperation, guilt, fear—that cannot be denied even if the most skeptical among us insist on denying the reality or truth of the ghost itself. Those who are intent on "proving" or "disproving" the ghosts may well miss this point and, in so doing, misunderstand the authenticity of these experiences. What things are is far less important than what things mean, and meaning emerges from the minded ways that people act toward things and the consequences thereof. The reality and truth of ghosts not only can be understood as emerging from these actions and intense human dramas but are often also, and more importantly, *inseparable* from them. In other words, the highly emotional—sometimes tearful—accounts of ghostly encounters are frequently as haunting as the ghosts themselves, and their source has as much to do with ghostly reason as it does with the uncanny.

A GHOSTLY EDGE

Twenty-year-old Brian enjoys "legend tripping" with his friends—visiting the site of a legend in the hope of experiencing a supernatural encounter (Ellis 1993)—most often late at night or extremely early in the morning. At three o'clock on a November afternoon, he agrees to allow Michele and me into his home to hear about his many adventures. He rocks gently in an overstuffed easy chair, partially wrapped in a blanket, wearing sweatpants and a T-shirt but no socks or shoes. His greasy hair is a mess. Brian speaks in a groggy monotone that becomes animated only at climactic moments of his stories about various ghostly encounters. One of his ghostly destinations near his small hometown is an abandoned house in the middle of a farmer's field. It was once the home of an abusive, alcoholic "guy that would come home, kick open the door, and yell, 'Bitch, I'm home!'" Brian says. He is fuzzy about the details, admitting that he and his friends "don't know what happened," only that the obnoxious guy and his wife "were found dead there one day." Brian and his friends now believe the abandoned home is haunted.

Brian continues to rock slowly in his chair as he explains, "We went out there, and one of my friends kicked open the door—he actually busted the door to the point that it wouldn't latch anymore—and he said, 'Bitch, we're here!'" Moments later, they entered the abandoned home, and

> me and two other people looked off to our right, and we saw a woman sitting there with her finger up to her lip as if to tell us to be quiet. I'm like, "That's creepy as hell!" I then looked down and saw this face covered in blood—a human face, a man's face—covered in blood just staring at me. Then it disappeared.

Brian and his friends fled, leaving the abandoned home a little worse for wear, although they would return again. On another visit, after again kicking the door and yelling, "Bitch, we're here!" they walked into the abandoned home to see "a bottle just floating in midair," Brian says, then tilting back "like someone was drinking from it. And then it just fell and shattered." On yet another visit, one of his friends lost his cell phone and, after much searching, finally found it

leaning against the wall where they believe the woman of the house was murdered. Although the friend was "thankful he got his phone back," according to Brian, "for some reason he got the feeling that something was wrong with the phone." Upon inspecting its contents, the friends found inexplicable "pictures of an entity on it, and then a picture of the face exactly as I saw [it] covered in blood. It's creepy."

The abandoned house, however, is not Brian's favorite place to legend trip. Indeed, Brian becomes a bit more animated as he talks about a short segment of a rural road that runs by an old cemetery. Inside the cemetery "you hear people talking, and there's nobody out there," he says. "You hear chains rattling, dogs barking, footsteps, twigs snapping—and the sounds get closer and closer to you. Weird stuff happens out there." The road itself, at least in the vicinity of the cemetery, is equally believed to be haunted. "One time we were out there, just driving, and out of nowhere this black truck appeared—out of nowhere!" he says. "It just randomly showed up in front of us, and then it disappeared." Brian explains the legend of the haunted cemetery and adjacent road, using curiously similar language and themes:

> There was a lady, a guy, and their three kids that used to live out there. [The lady and the guy] went out one evening, and when they returned, two of their kids were brutally murdered, and her baby was taken. A note was left behind saying, "Bitch, I have your baby." Now if you drive down that road and you say that, it pisses her off. . . . [T]hey say she killed herself—hung herself—because she couldn't find her baby. And she's still trying to find her baby. Now she appears as either the "lady in white" or the "lady in red." The "lady in white" is more reasonable, but when she is red, you don't wanna piss her off.

Brian and his friends frequently visit this area, where he has seen "orbs—blue, green, and red orbs," as well as "an apparition of a little kid being hanged from a tree." In fact, the young men—who seem to lose their phones frequently—have had many harrowing experiences on and around the haunted road and cemetery, according to Brian. They

> have been pushed, shoved, scraped—had marks on 'em! One other time I was out there with my friends and one of them got pushed against the van, and it took me and two of my friends to pull him off. Our feet were even on the van, and we couldn't pull him off no matter what we did. Another time we were out there, and a friend of mine lost his phone. We were about a quarter mile from the cemetery, and his phone just disappeared.

We called his phone, and we could hear it out in the woods, so we went looking. Then we couldn't hear it anymore. We drove around a bit, and all of a sudden we could hear his phone in the cemetery. We drove out to the cemetery again but couldn't hear it anymore. So we called it one more time, sayin', "If we can't find it, then we are just gonna leave." And there it was—his phone was behind the wheel of the van.

Brian is looking forward to the change of season, because "when you go out there in the winter, you see piles of dead rats—which I'm hoping to see when I go back out there next. It's one of the worst places I've ever been to."

Unlike anyone else we encountered, Brian has had many experiences with at least moderately menacing specters. But then, also unlike anyone else we spoke to, Brian actively seeks out ghosts whom he boldly taunts. Brian even desires to be possessed by a ghost. "I wanna experience being taken over," he says, adding, "I want to experience it myself just to see what it's like. You know, but if I get fully taken over, there's a chance of not coming back. But I just think it would be fun, something to experience."

Brian gives the appearance of being cool and careless, yet he repeatedly states that these ghostly encounters make him "feel uneasy" and frequently "terrified." Perplexed, I can't help but question him. "Then why do you keep going back to these places?" I ask, no doubt with a puzzled look on my face. Brian responds listlessly:

Why not? It gives me something to do. I mean, I'm terrified of that stuff, but it still intrigues me. So I just go out there. Just the fact that, although I might be afraid of it, but it's still kinda cool experiencing that—even though you are terrified. I wanna experience it myself just to see what it's like.

Brian's answer seems unsatisfying, even ridiculous. But like many things, his reply makes better sense in the broader context of his life. Michele and I interviewed Brian in the basement of his mother's house, where he had been living since high school graduation two and a half years earlier. After making one unsuccessful attempt to gain admission to the local community college, he showed no further interest. He spent months playing videogames as most of his friends moved away to attend colleges, universities, or technical schools. Brian finally got a job at a gas station convenience store, but it didn't last long; he was fired after a few months. Shortly after he lost the job, Brian also lost his automobile, which could not withstand the cruelties of his driving. He was unemployed for many months before he eventually landed another job, at a local fast food restaurant, where he had managed to stay employed for about six months—although he still had to borrow a car from his parents to get to work.

Brian's love life mirrored his work history: more off than on, and still nothing long term. He had no career aspirations or educational, technical, or vocational ambitions. Aside from videogames, Brian had no hobbies or any other kind of recreational pastimes. Seen in this light, Brian's ghostly legend tripping was not only "something to do" but also one of the small ways that he pushed an "edge," asserting himself as a unique and independent person. It was, perhaps, one of his few resources for doing so.

"Edgework," wrote Stephen Lyng (1990: 882), is "a type of experiential anarchy in which the individual moves beyond the realm of established social patterns to the very fringes of ordered reality." Edgework is classically understood in the context of activities such as skydiving, bungee-cord jumping, extreme sports, and other, similar voluntary risk-taking activities. And while each form of edgework has unique characteristics, all forms have features in common, including "the problem of negotiating the boundary between chaos and order" in the context of a "clearly observable threat to one's physical or mental well-being or one's sense of an ordered existence" whereby edgeworkers "avoid being paralyzed by fear" to "maintain control over a situation that verges on complete chaos." Edgework entails a "magnified sense of self" in that having "survived the challenge, one feels capable of dealing with any threatening situation." In this way, edgework "is a rational and therapeutic way to respond to a sense of helplessness" (Lyng 1990: 855, 859–860, 874).

Brian, it would seem, lives on many edges. Yet his active pursuits of ghostly experiences are, perhaps, among the sparse resources he has for "direct personal authorship" of his actions to call out "an anarchic self in which ego is manifest but the personal, institutional self is completely suppressed" (Lyng 1990: 878). In the words of Marina

Warner (1998: 6), Brian pursues frightening ghostly encounters "not only as a source of pleasure but as a means of strengthening the sense of being alive, or having a command over self." It is the languid specter of Brian's everyday life that haunts in ways that surpass the ghosts that he seeks out as remedial medication: a lackluster everyday life that is empty of aspiration and motivation and that is deficient in both social capital and personal resources for achievement and accomplishment. Neither the will to believe nor ghostly reason can account for Brian's experiences. While others we spoke to struggled with or against the will to believe, for Brian ghostly encounters are more about a will to be.

3

GHOSTLY TOPOLOGY

Ghostly encounters are extremely diverse. The people in this study described an enormous range of experiences in which a presence was seen, heard, felt, or smelled or some combination thereof.[1] Ghostly encounters may be experienced as random or reoccurring, fleeting or enduring, chaotic or predictable. There is no simple, general formula to the ghostly experiences that people report. There are, however, general patterns that are helpful for *classification*. Grouping and naming things according to common characteristics is a helpful strategy to identify patterns, although we should be careful, because having a label for something doesn't necessarily mean that we understand any better.

In this chapter I provide a classification framework for the ghostly encounters reported in this research. Because our objectives are classificatory, this chapter is not only primarily descriptive but also risks citing a greater abundance of data to better illustrate the rich diversity of ghostly experiences. I must emphasize that this classifi-

---

1. Of all of our major extrospective senses, taste appears to be the only one that people do not commonly report perceiving a ghostly presence.

cation framework is based entirely on data we collected; there may be other forms and types, and we do not claim that our framework is comprehensive. I begin with a helpful distinction between *types of hauntings* and *forms of ghosts*. Without exception, each of the ninety-one reported experiences with ghosts in this research fell into one or more of these types and forms.[2] I follow with a discussion of two common characteristics—one a fascinating aspect of ghosts themselves, and the other a product of taken-for-granted human interpretation. The chapter concludes with rare accounts of truly terrifying experiences.

TYPES OF HAUNTINGS

I use the term "haunting" to refer to the general characteristics of a ghostly encounter—the conditions, circumstances, and overall demeanor of the specific forms of ghosts that appear (described in the next section). Four types of hauntings are evident in the data reported. The first two types of hauntings, intelligent and residual, are mutually exclusive, and all hauntings appear to be one or the other. The other two types, anniversary and historical, are much less common, but having appeared a few times in this research, they deserve a brief comment.[3]

---

2. Seventy-one people participated in this research. Collectively, the participants in this study described a total of ninety-one hauntings involving 144 distinct ghosts. Admittedly, these are difficult to quantify. Sometimes people reported prolonged uncanny experiences (over the course of months, years, and even decades) that they attributed to a single ghostly presence. In other instances, they perceived multiple encounters as separate ghostly presences. I took what people said at face value and counted them accordingly. For more discussion of methods, data, and analysis, see the Appendix.

3. The low number of anniversary and historical hauntings in the study is likely the result of a selection bias. We focused on "everyday ghosts" and, in fact, intentionally avoided other genres of ghostly encounters, such as "commercial ghosts," "professionalized ghosts," and "institutional ghosts." (Those genres are discussed in Chapter 5.) Other kinds of ghostly encounters may contain much more frequent anniversary and historical hauntings, especially the genre we call "institutional ghosts."

Intelligent Hauntings

The basic distinction between "intelligent" and "residual" hauntings is common knowledge among paranormal investigators and ghost enthusiasts. An intelligent haunting is defined as a ghostly presence that interacts with the environment, living people, or both. Those interactions are taken to signify that the ghost is aware of the living world, even self-aware, and hence "intelligent." The majority of the hauntings reported in this research were intelligent (76 percent). Interaction, the crucial sign of an intelligent haunting, is broadly defined but can be separated into direct interactions with living people and indirect interactions with objects in the environment.

Some intelligent hauntings entail *direct* interaction with living people in the form of vocalizations or some kind of immediate somatic impression. Of the two, vocalization, and especially speech, is less common; only rarely do ghosts speak. Allison, age sixteen, recalled in great detail her experience with a talking ghost she first encountered the day her family moved into a home of their own. She heard a noise coming from her brothers' bedroom, opened the closet door, and saw the apparition of a young girl with brown hair, dressed in vintage clothing. Before she vanished, the young girl said, "My name is Madison. This is my house."[4] From then on, Allison had many conversations with the ghost in the closet, but that is unusual. When ghosts speak, they seldom utter more than a simple word, name, or phrase, as the following respondents reported:

> The first winter that we lived here, we had some friends over. They were standing in the entry right over there [*motioning to the front door*]. They were leaving, and from the kitchen we heard a little girl say, "Goodbye." There was nobody in the kitchen. (Brooke, age twenty-six)

---

4. Of the four closet ghosts in this study, all but one was a child, although the one exception wasn't exactly a closet ghost, either: the informant reported seeing the apparition of a man simply standing in the *doorway* of her closet.

My boyfriend slept over one night. He got up in the middle of the night to go to the bathroom, and as he was crossing the stairs at two or three in the morning, he heard a whispered, "Hey!" coming from the bottom of the stairs. That really freaked me out, cuz I was, like, "Now we are hearing voices in my house. So maybe there really is something going on here." (Paige, age twenty-five)

Sometimes I'd be just sitting there, or lying down, and all of a sudden there would be this voice say[ing], "Grace!" [*in a sharp whisper*]. I could feel the breath on my ear, and I'd be, like, "Holy shit!" and freak out. (Grace, age forty-eight)

Frequently, when ghosts are reported to vocalize, it is a nonlingual expression of an emotional state, such as crying, screaming, or moaning. For five years, Amy, age nineteen, had worked as a nanny in a house in which both she and the parents who employed her heard crying. "We'd often hear the crying," Amy told me, "then go check on the infants, and nothing. We just got used to it. We called it a ghost baby." Others reported similar kinds of nonlingual vocalizations:

My cousin and I were playing upstairs, . . . and we heard what we thought was a whisper. We both stopped, and my cousin turned to me and said, "Did you hear that?" I said, "Yeah! I thought I was hearing things." All of a sudden, a middle-age-sounding woman just started screaming. It sounded like she was in the room—it didn't sound like it was outside or anything. Just ballistically screaming at us. (Vicki, age nineteen)

I often hear a woman crying in the stairway going upstairs. (Mike, age twenty-one)

My father then heard a girl-like blood-curdling scream that was right into his ear. [It was] so loud and startling that he instantly fell to his knees and covered his ears. (Susie, age twenty)

When people reported experiences of nonvocal direct interaction in an intelligent haunting, it took the form of immediate somatic impressions—tugs, pushes, taps, distinct odors, and sometimes an electrical or choking sensation. These direct physical sensations were distinctly experienced but had no observable source or cause:

> About three weeks ago, I was sleeping and my feet were hanging over the bed. I woke up to the feeling that someone was pressing on my foot—I mean, like, three times. I woke up, looked down, and nothing was there. All the cats were sleeping next to me; nothing was on the floor. Nothing. (Tara, age twenty-seven)

> Something came and hit me in the back. You know, just kinda pushed me. I have not been touched before [by a ghost], but I definitely felt something push me. (Martha, age sixty-one)

> I felt the same sensation as, like, when a kid tugs at your pants to get your attention. Obviously, I turned around, and nothing was there. (Josh, age twenty-three)

> It stops you in your tracks. I don't know how to explain that feeling. It's cool and almost takes your breath away. You feel suddenly alert—very aware of your surroundings. Almost an electrical feel, like static. (Leslie, age thirty-five)

> I could smell the Ivory soap she always used. It was very soothing, and I was at peace. (Lana, age fifty-seven)

> It was during the middle of the night when I woke up to something grabbing my ankle and pulling me down the bed. (Elise, age twenty-four)

Most frequently, intelligent hauntings entail *indirect* interaction in which objects in the environment are inexplicably manipulated: doors open or close, electrical devices operate erratically, items move, something makes the sound of footsteps on floors or stairs or bangs or knocks on windows and doors. For example, Lindsey, age twenty-one, recalled sitting on her bed reading a book with the closet to her left. The closet door was open. "All of a sudden, the clothes in my closet started moving," Lindsey said. "It was like a hand swept across my clothes and just pushed them, and they were swaying and swaying back and forth." This kind of indirect interaction, in which a ghostly presence is perceived to manipulate objects in an environment, is the most common form of interaction that qualifies as an intelligent haunting:

> My brother was watching TV and the remote on the coffee table started moving, maybe an inch at a time slowly. At one point, it just shot across the coffee table onto the floor. The batteries flew out of it. Basically it exploded all over the floor. (Diane, age twenty)

> The lights would flicker at night as the pots and pans in the kitchen would rattle. (Tiffany, age thirty-eight)

> The water would turn on in the bathtub in the middle of the night. It was just [*pause and deep sigh*], it was really nonstop. It happened all the time, and we never had explanations. (Nikki, age eighteen)

> My thermostat kept turning itself down to sixty. First it was happening maybe once a month. So you think, "Yeah, I must have bumped it." Then I started noticing it happening more frequently. It was always at sixty, and I would say it was happening every couple of hours. It just kept turning down. (Martha, age sixty-one)

> It's just all the banging and knocking! It knocks from the second floor window—knocking from the outside where it is physically impossible for someone to be. Sometimes we will see a dark shadow through the window or just hear the knocking. (Dylan, age thirty-five)

> We have a cabinet between my parents' bedroom, my sister's bedroom, and my bedroom. [The ghost] would always open the cabinets like he was looking for something. (Amy, age nineteen)

In cases of direct and indirect interaction, intelligent hauntings entail a lot of physical activity that appears deliberate and attention seeking, and is sometimes experienced with maddening frequency. Grace, age forty-eight, lived in a home where she and her daughter experienced uncanny, irritating, and unnerving events so often that she ultimately left the house simply to be rid of the harassment. Grace described some of the perpetual uncanny happenings that she lived with for four months:

> I'd go to bed and I'd hear the sound of all the glasses in the kitchen breaking, and I'd go out there and there'd be nothing. I used to collect music boxes, and it got to where they would all just start playing. They'd just start playing randomly. Then we had this shelf—it was about six feet tall and five feet wide— and it was full of knickknacks and stuff. Three times we came home and the shelf was off the wall and on the other side of the room, but everything in the shelf was sitting exactly where it was supposed to be—as nice as could be. And the fourth time that happened everything was shattered and broken. Another time I woke up in the middle of the night, and all of my dirty clothes were in a pile on the floor in the middle of my room. So, yeah, it was just random weird shit, and I don't know how else to explain it. It really was strange.

On rare occasions, people reported intelligent hauntings in which the ghost appeared like a living person and the interaction was identical to how living people interact with one another. While accounts of this kind of interaction rarely appeared in our research, these kinds of ghostly encounters were once quite common (see Clarke 2012), and such ghostly presences are the main feature of reported encounters with ghostly hitchhikers (see Jones 1959). Of all of the people who shared their ghostly encounters with us, those who reported experiencing a ghost that appeared no different from a living person provided the richest, most vivid, and most detailed descriptions. Several accounts of lifelike ghosts and direct interactions that closely approximated interactions with living people are described elsewhere in this book; for now, we illustrate this phenomenon by citing experiences reported by Kimberly, age twenty-two.

As a young girl, Kimberly attended an auction with the rest of her immediate and extended family to liquidate the estate of a distant relative. "They owned an old farmhouse and auctioned off all the property that they had," Kimberly recalled. "I had never been to the house before." During the auction, Kimberly said, her parents "set me loose on the farm to just roam around and play." She fondly recalled "playing with this little girl for the whole day. We just played around the yard, and around back by the barn." Although they were playmates only for that one day, Kimberly said she would never forget what the girl looked like: "pale, but she had really long, dark brown, curly hair. I thought it was just the prettiest thing I've ever seen. And she had such striking blue eyes." Kimberly concluded her description by stating for a third time, "I'll never forget it." The rest of Kimberly's family, however, had no memory of what her auction-day playmate looked like because they couldn't see her at all. Kimberly said:

> My mom finally called me back over to her, and she asked what I was doing. I explained to her who I was playing with, and she said, "Oh, an imaginary friend?" I got super-pissed cuz I was, like, "No, she's not fake." I got really mad. So my mom tried playing along and asked, "So what does she look like?" I spewed off everything I could remember about the girl.

Kimberly's aunt, who was standing next to her mother, listened carefully to the description, went into the farmhouse, and came back out with an old family portrait, Kimberly said, asking:

> "Do you recognize the girl on here?" I pointed out the girl in the picture that I was playing with, and my aunt got super-freaked out. Apparently, the girl in the picture, who I was playing with all day, died when she was seven. She was buried in the front yard underneath the oak tree, because this family buried their family members in the front yard at that time.

Intelligent hauntings are the most common reported in this study. Intelligent hauntings entail ghosts that interact with the environment, the people within it, or both. Some reports of intelligent hauntings involved ghosts that interact in a manner that is no different from how living people interact with one another, but in most cases the interaction is ephemeral. Sometimes that ephemeral interaction is direct—occasionally speech, nonlingual vocalizations, or a somatic impression. Most often that ephemeral interaction is indirect and through explicable manipulations of objects in the environment.

Residual Hauntings

A residual haunting entails a ghostly presence that does not interact with its environment or living occupants. Residual hauntings appeared less frequently in the data we collected (24 percent). We found two major forms of residual hauntings. The first, and most common, was a single, fleeting, and isolated uncanny event that was indifferent to the environment or people within it. For example:

> We could hear the front door open and close. When we went to look, there was no one out there. But it sounded like someone was coming into the house. (Lana, age fifty-seven)[5]

> We saw a shadow in the basement. It was on a wall and probably about eight feet high. The big shadow moved right across the wall. (Vicki, age nineteen)

The classic definition of a residual haunting involves people seeing or hearing a ghostly presence repeatedly and in the exact the same manner.[6] For example, Luke, age twenty-seven, said that he grew up in a house where "all the time I would hear footsteps coming down the steps, walking through the playroom that was downstairs, and

---

5. This is a helpful example of the difference between intelligent and residual hauntings; had the door actually opened and closed, we would have classified it as an intelligent haunting, because the ghost was reported to have interacted with the physical environment.

6. Because of this, paranormal investigators and ghost enthusiasts often do not consider residuals true haunting. Rather than a ghostly presence with a will and volition of its own, residuals are frequently regarded as a kind of inexplicable recorded playback of events that previously occurred. For this research, we did not treat residual hauntings any differently from intelligent ones.

then walk right alongside my bed, and then walk back up the steps." Luke remembered this pattern of footsteps occurring repeatedly: "the same thing over and over; just pacing back and forth all night."

These repeating patterns—as if something were stuck in a "*compulsion to repeat*" (Freud 2003 [1919]: 145)—are frequently regarded as a common characteristic of residual hauntings. In our research, however, we found only two reported instances of this kind of repetitive residual haunting. All of the other residual hauntings were of apparitions, shadows, mists, and orbs with uncanny characteristics but that otherwise did not interact with people or the environment.

Anniversary and Historical Hauntings

We encountered two other types of hauntings in this research—anniversary and historical hauntings—but both were relatively uncommon. An anniversary haunting entails witnessing a ghostly presence on (or very close to) the date of a specific or corresponding event of significance to the ghost. For example, an anniversary ghost may appear on the date of his or her death or birth or on an annual holiday. Our research suggests that anniversary ghosts are more common in popular culture than in everyday life, and people appear to expect anniversary ghosts more often than they are actually experienced. Lee's encounter with an apparition on his twenty-first birthday in the same room where a former resident died of alcohol poisoning on her twenty-first birthday (see Chapter 2) could be considered an anniversary haunting. Krystal, age twenty-three, provided a better example:

> My best friend killed himself on May 7, 2009. He did it at 4:40 A.M., just minutes after talking to me [on the phone]. In the summer of 2009, precisely one month after—precisely to the day—I woke up and thought I was seeing white lights, like reflections on a white wall, but kind of blurry. I kept waking up and seeing them, waking up and seeing them. When I woke up the final time, I looked at my phone and saw it was June 7, 4:40 A.M., and I all of a sudden felt a warm, peaceful, comforting sensation. I know it was John.

Paranormal investigators and ghost enthusiasts often claim that anniversary ghosts are almost universally intelligent hauntings. All of the anniversary ghosts reported in this study were intelligent, but they were too few in number to allow for much comment.

Historical hauntings appear in places of historical significance in which people primarily report seeing apparitions. When they are seen in a human form, they are typically wearing period-appropriate clothing or uniforms. Vicki, age nineteen, said:

> I got out of the car and looked up the hill, and I saw fifteen or so colonial-dressed people standing there. I looked away and then looked back, and they were all gone. I saw men and women of all ages, but mostly middle age—not too many younger or older. . . . [L]ater that night we went home, and one of the guys that was with us did some research on the area— the hanging that happened there. According to legend, the one hundred or so people that watched the hanging were doomed to roam [the area]. I just chalk it up to that and feel that the fifteen or so people I saw in the hill were those spectators of the hanging.

Paranormal investigators and ghost enthusiasts typically claim that historical hauntings are almost always residual. All of the historical hauntings in this study were residual, but they were also too few in number to allow for much comment.

FORMS OF GHOSTS

The people we spoke to identified ninety-one distinct hauntings that included a total of 144 ghosts. Those ghosts appeared in a variety of forms, and we identify six: apparitions, phantasms, wraiths, poltergeists, specters, and phantoms. These forms, however, are not mutually exclusive. All 144 reports of ghosts in this study fell into at least one of these six forms, and, as we illustrate, some reported experiences had characteristics of more than one form.[7]

---

7. Thus, the overall percentages we report do not add up to one hundred.

Apparitions

The word "appear"—to come into sight; to become visible—is the root of "apparition." Thus, an apparition implies an evanescent visual presence that approximates something physical or material. Similarly, we use the word "apparition" to refer to visible ghosts, ghosts that are seen. Sixty-five of the 144 ghostly encounters in this research (45 percent) were with apparitions.[8] Amy, age nineteen, gave a clear example:

> I remember one night, I was sleeping downstairs with a bunch of my girlfriends—you know, the whole slumber party whatever. And I remember waking up in the middle of the night and had the need to look over to my left and I saw this [*pause*]—it was a male—fuzzy, white-gray. And I remember waking them up and [saying], like, "Dude, someone's down here!" They all started laughing at me because they obviously didn't see him. . . . I know that I saw someone, or something, and he was gone after that. He had broad shoulders; he looked like he had—not puffy hair but mid-, above-ear hair. I couldn't see his clothes, but I could tell that it was just a T-shirt. Flowy bottom. I mean, not anything weird, but I could tell that it wasn't a girly figure. T-shirt and the bottom was kinda just [*pause*] there, fuzzed out. . . . [H]e was all white, I could just see his outline and that was it. Just standing there, hanging out, doing nothing. Then he was gone. Completely just [*pause*] boom, disappeared.

Amy recalled seeing the apparition of a man. Likewise, reports of apparitions most frequently involved seeing a human form—either partial (as in Amy's account) or complete. Forty-four of the sixty-five accounts of apparitions (68 percent) in the study involved seeing a human form of some kind, often quite vividly. For example, Maggie, age twenty, said that she grew up in an "old house and, in my bedroom, I would open the closet and there would be a little boy sit-

---

8. When people think about ghosts, most often they imagine apparitions. It is worth noting that only about half of all ghostly encounters reported in this study involved a visible presence of any kind.

ting there. He had short brunette hair, always wearing a plain shirt and jeans. He would always tell me, 'My name is Quimby.'" Maggie clearly remembers this apparition, mainly because she encountered him often. "I saw Quimby a lot," Maggie said. "My parents would often see me talking to him. Of course, no one believed me, cuz, like, "Oh kids! Whatever" [*in a dismissive tone*]." But I remember specifically what he looked like and that he was in my closet all the time."

Many of the reports of human apparitions involve equally vivid details. For example:

During the middle of the night I woke up. I saw a middle-aged woman with brunette hair sitting on the right side of my bed staring at me. I saw her for about three seconds and she disappeared. (Elise, age twenty-four)

I saw an adult male figure come in [my bedroom], wearing a light-green short-sleeved shirt, and he had light skin. He touched my hips in a way of sympathy, walked toward the window, and vanished. (Claire, age twenty)

We see a little girl in pajamas, too—really specifically detailed. . . . I have a little display of golf balls outside my office, and she will knock those off, tip the clubs, knock things over—almost as if to drive me absolutely crazy. Most recently, my best friend told me he saw a young girl in pajamas standing in my office doorway. (Dylan, age thirty-five)

My sister saw a lady in a red dress singing. My uncle who lives downstairs saw a really pretty lady down there, too. But when I see her, she's not a beautiful lady—just a typical-looking one. She's usually seen singing or just walking around. Once my sister heard singing downstairs through the vent and thought it was my uncle, but he wasn't home the whole weekend. (Ella, age twenty)

Thirty of the human apparitions in this study were adults (68 percent of the apparitions), twelve were children (27 percent), and the remaining two involved a group of apparitions of mixed ages (e.g.,

Vicki's account of the historical haunting cited earlier). Of the forty-four accounts of human apparitions, thirty indicated a gender, and the distribution was split almost evenly between men (47 percent) and women (53 percent).

Twenty-one accounts of apparitions involved seeing something nonhuman. Fourteen of those reports (67) entailed seeing eerie shadows. Paige, age twenty-five, provided one of the richest examples:

> I would see shadows moving in the room. . . . I'd never seen darkness like that before. I used to feel comfort in the darkness. I was used to the darkness. I liked being in darkness. But this darkness scared me. It was so dense that I couldn't see through it at all—that's how dark it was. Even with the moonlight, outside lights, clock lights, and everything else, I couldn't see certain areas of my room cuz it was so dense.

Aaron, age twenty-three, also saw strange shadows over the course of several days, although unlike in Paige's experience, the shadows followed Aaron around. He said:

> I started to see these shadows. When it started, they would hover across the room and stuff. I thought my eyes were just playing tricks on me. But then, as the days went on, I would always see one directly to the left of me, and it was shorter. There was a taller one to my right.

Popular media is saturated with ghostly orbs and mists, especially in photos that purport to have captured apparitions. In our research, people reported orbs and mists only occasionally. In fact, we found only four ghostly encounters of mist or orb apparitions. "I wasn't sure as to what I was seeing," said Lana, age fifty-seven, as she described the ghostly mist she observed, "but it wasn't walking on the ground." Instead, she said, "It was floating. It was light blue with illuminating flowing colors of white and blue. It seemed to flow in the wind, of which there wasn't much that night." The colorful mist disappeared into the barn on Lana's farm, never to be seen again. Although this happened infrequently, others did report similar fleeting encounters with reclusive mists and orbs:

Right at the foot of my bed there was this misty white thing. It came at me, and it wasn't like it was going to hurt me. Still, I screamed because I didn't know what it was. It was really weird, because it wasn't like a figure—not like a person or anything—just a misty white thing. (Samantha, age forty-two)

When my husband moved in, he would notice things, as well. The biggest thing that happened to him is when we would sleep and at night he would wake up to a white light circling above our bed. He would get really freaked out by that. I didn't believe him and what he was telling me. But one night he woke me up and I saw it. It didn't last long, but it was kinda like a white circle, maybe the size of a golf ball—almost smoky, like you could see through it—and it just spun in a circle really fast above our bed, and then it was gone. (Tiffany, age thirty-eight)

About half of all ghostly encounters were of apparitions, and the majority (68 percent) reported seeing a human form. Reports of nonhuman apparitions involved mostly eerie shadows (22 percent), followed by a small number of experiences with mists and orbs. Our data contain only three reports of apparitions that appeared to be non-human but were not shadows, mists, or orbs. They all were apparitions of companion animals—one dog and two cats —that reportedly visited their owners shortly after they died.

Phantasms

All of the sixty-five reports of apparitions in this study appeared to people when they were fully conscious. In some instances (just eight, or 6 percent, in this research), people reported seeing a ghostly presence in a dream or another altered state of awareness. We did not count these experiences as apparitions; instead, were refer to them as phantasms. With apparitions, people are reasonably confident of what they saw or remember having seen. They are less certain about what they experience in dreams and other altered states of awareness. Thus, we use the term "phantasm" to signify the illusionary nature of what is reflected in the reported data. Diane, age twenty, for example, reported three distinct ghostly encounters. She was certain that in her first experience she saw an apparition: "I saw a figure, and it was, like, very, *very* visible. I could *easily* see it." But she qualified the second experience by saying, "I didn't really see a ghost. It was actually a dream." This is precisely the kind of distinction people frequently made, prompting us to treat phantasms as distinct forms. Diane continued:

> The dream was this last year. It was with my dad's dad, who has passed. He came to me in my dream and told me that he needed me to pass on a message to my grandmother, who is still alive. He said, "It's very important. Don't forget." So I was, like, "OK." And he said, "Just tell her that it's going to be OK. Don't be sad," and he is all right.

Diane woke up "kinda confused," she said, and decided to call her father and ask him whether her grandmother was OK. He said she was, as far as he knew, and suggested Diane call her grandmother. Heeding her father, Diane says she made the call and recounted:

> I told her what my grandpa said to tell her. She was really confused, and I think, if anything, she was ticked off at me for even bringing him up and saying something weird like that. The next week, her cat—which actually my grandpa adopted from a shelter—passed away. That cat was very significant to my grandma, a huge symbol of my grandpa to her. So that was a huge loss for her. I feel like that was what my grandpa was trying to tell her: that the cat was going to pass away, and that it's going to be OK.

The people in our study seldom reported experiences with phantasms, and that's understandable. In dreams and other altered states of awareness, people routinely see and experience things that they most often understand to be products of their own minds. The experience may be pleasurable, terrifying, strange, awkward, or even mundane. But with the exception of a few psychoanalysts and psychedelic mind trippers, people seldom take the content of these altered states of mind seriously. Something else has to happen for people to report experiences with phantasms—as in Diane's account, in which a dream involving her deceased grandfather was followed by the death of a beloved pet—and that is consistent with the process by which uncanny events become ghosts (see Chapter 2).

Ella, age twenty, provided another example:

> I started dreaming about a ghost that lives in my closet. She's a redhead, Caucasian—but she's handicapped; she walks crippled. In my dream, she came out of the closet and into my room and told me that this is her area, that she is sad, and she lives here, too. So that happened in my dream, and I woke up frightened. . . . [A]gain I would dream about this person in my closet. But this time I dreamed that I actually spoke to my closet, telling that person to move on to the next life just because this isn't where she belongs. [In my dream] I poked a broomstick into the closet, and all of a sudden I could see her head poking out—just her head—and she wouldn't look at me or anything. . . . [L]ater, when we were cleaning the room, we found red hair on the floor, and I thought, "That's weird. We don't have red hair. None of our friends have red hair, either."

As Diane's and Ella's experiences illustrate, a dream is just a dream until something else happens. Experiences with phantasms emerge from coinciding life events for which simple coincidence is hard to accept. This is often the case, for example, in experiences of a phantasm that we call a wraith, although not all wraiths are phantasms.

Wraiths

Traditionally defined, a "wraith" is a known person who visits the living around the time of his or her death. That is precisely how we use the term. In the data we collected, accounts of wraiths universally featured deceased loved ones; they portended the death and comforted the living. For example, Karen, age twenty-one, recalled her experience with a wraith:

> I was in the fifth grade, so I'm assuming I was around ten or eleven. [Grandma] was on a machine keeping her alive at home. The doctor came over while my family all stood around

her and he shut off the machine. It was a very traumatizing moment for us being so young, but my mom thought we would want to be there. We all sat around [Grandma] while she slowly slipped away. Once she had, I felt something touch my shoulder, and I turned around and it was a faint image of my grandma. I thought I was just seeing things, but each one of us in the room felt and saw the same thing. My grandma probably was just trying to comfort us and let us know that she was going to be OK.

Consistent with Karen's experience, wraiths are commonly either apparitions or phantasms, since some kind of visual confirmation of the (soon to be) deceased loved one was present in almost all of the accounts we collected:

When my dad died, I was in my apartment, and my daughter was, oh, maybe a week and a half old. I walked out of my bedroom and saw my dad sitting at my dining room table, just looking at me. He was just sitting there. (Grace, age forty-eight)

I found myself sobbing and drenching my pillow with my tears. My mother was suddenly there, in the room with me. She placed her soft, warm hand on mine, which was still on my chest. She said "Oh, honey, it's going to be OK. Stop crying now. It's going to be OK." (Lana, age fifty-seven)

Reports of wraith experiences were not common in our research. In fact, wraiths accounted for only five of the 144 reported ghosts (3 percent).

Poltergeists

Geist is the German word for "ghost," and *poltern* means to crash about, bang, or otherwise make noise. Hence, a literal definition of "poltergeist" is "noisy ghost"—one that makes its presence known mainly through inexplicable sounds. I have chosen to broaden this literal definition. Poltergeists make their presence known primarily through baffling sounds, but also by moving objects, turning electrical devices on and off, opening and closing doors, and manipulating other physical objects in the environment:

> We hear that kind of stuff often—like, things falling to the floor, but nothing's fallen. Or when I'm down here on the main floor, I hear footsteps—people walking around. It sounds like there's a bunch of people walking around upstairs. (Brooke, age twenty-six)

> I was getting ready in the bathroom with the door closed when all of a sudden it began to slowly open and then close again by itself. (Donna, age twenty-one)

> We were sitting at our dining room table, and my entire family witnessed this box move across the kitchen counter by itself. It just slowly slid across the counter. (Nikki, age eighteen)

> I mean, just weird things would happen. Like, at Christmastime I was sitting on the couch in the living room, and in the bookcase—which was six feet from the couch, approximately—I had an old mercury ornament. . . . I was sitting on the couch having my morning coffee, and the ornament came out of the bookcase, dangled for a while in the air, fell on the carpet, and broke into a million pieces. (Beth, age sixty-six)

> I had a TV in my bedroom. I was sleeping, and everything was off. All of a sudden the TV turned on and the channels started randomly flipping, all on its own. The remote was on the floor next to my bed; nothing was touching it—the dog wasn't even in my room. I don't know how, but the TV just turned on and was flipping channels. (Sarah, age twenty-eight)

Poltergeists accounted for forty-six of the 144 ghosts reported in this study (32 percent). As the quotes below illustrate, of the six ghostly forms we identified, poltergeists had the most consistent and stable characteristics. The poltergeists in this study were almost universally place-bound; they haunted specific buildings, mostly homes and sometimes explicitly one space within a home. Poltergeists were associated with an enormous range of strange noises and physical activity, but they almost never appeared as apparitions. Other ghostly forms were mostly experienced as isolated, fleeting events; poltergeists, by contrast, were persistent. People frequently reported experiencing a poltergeist over the course of months, years, and even decades. Whereas reported encounters with other ghostly forms are not (or cannot be) corroborated by others, poltergeists were most often experienced by multiple people who reported the same uncanny happenings over time. Finally, people often reported feeling startled, even annoyed, by poltergeists—but almost never threatened by them.

Participants in our study reported a total of fifteen haunted houses, and all except one described characteristic poltergeist activity. Moreover, in ten of the fifteen accounts of haunted houses, the informants specifically identified some kind of home renovation as the moment in which strange things started to occur. For example, Martha, age sixty-one, pointed past her dining room table into the living room and commented, "We added that part of the house. . . . It was after that when I started noticing things happening in the house." Dylan, age thirty-five, also observed a correlation between home renovation and poltergeist activity, saying "The house I grew up in was built in, um, well sometime between 1890 and 1895. When I was really young, I didn't notice anything. But we put an addition on the house in 1986, I think it was, or maybe 1987. I never really noticed much until then." Other participants in the study, such as Lisa, age twenty-two, simply concluded, "It just seems like it isn't happy we're doing renovations on the house."

For years, Tiffany, age thirty-eight, experienced typical poltergeist activity in her home. "But just in the kitchen and dining room," she said. She offered an explanation that is consistent with what others have observed:

> I always thought, "Why is it always in there and not the bathroom or anywhere else?" But, then, the whole house had been redone—the carpet, the painting, the bathroom was redone— all of it except for the kitchen and dining room. Maybe it stays there because everything else had changed to something new.

Mischievousness is the most common characteristic of the poltergeist. "He feels like a jokester," said Amy, age nineteen, describing the character of the poltergeist she has been living with for years. "He takes stuff and hides it." She then described various objects that inexplicably disappeared, only to be found in peculiar places. Poltergeists are frequently described as tricksters that subject the living "to a wide variety of ghostly pranks" (Jones 1959: 63). Martha, age sixty-one, provided a good example of the kinds of pranks that are typical of poltergeists:

> I lost my glasses, which is not unusual for me to do because I don't need to wear them all the time. I could not find them. I finally found them in my bedroom, behind the door—you know, right in the corner there [*pointing toward her bedroom door*], standing straight on end, right up against the wall just like that [*motioning with her fingers*]. . . . [A]nd another time— I have toys that play musical things, but I don't have any toys that play "London Bridge Is Falling Down." One night I woke up hearing that song somewhere in the living room. Then the next night it was in my room, and as soon as I turned the light on, it stopped. The next night it kept playing after I turned the light on. I went to look for it, but I could not find it anywhere—and I knew I did not have a toy with that song. . . . My daughter and her friend were here, and they rented a few movies. They placed them on that table [*pointing to the dining room*], and they were in the living room the whole time. . . . [Later] we went over for the movies, and they weren't on the table. We looked all over. We could not find them. So I took the garbage out piece by piece, and there were those two movies at the very bottom. They couldn't have slipped through. I don't understand how they could move and no one saw them moving. And, you know, we have the usual things: TVs going on and off, lights going on and off.

Because experiences with poltergeists often occur over long periods of time, it is not unusual for people eventually to speak to these ghosts and sometimes try to rationalize with them. It took years for Nora, age forty-three, to reluctantly conclude that her house was haunted (see Chapter 2). Once she conceded that there was a ghost in her house after experiencing several unwanted uncanny events, she said, she decided to talk to the ghost to try to set some limits and boundaries. "At the end of the day—and it had been a very crazy day of renovation and remodeling—when it quieted down, I just went downstairs" and started a conversation:

> I said, "You know, I don't like change, either. I'm not very happy about needing to do this, to be honest. But I just want to tell you we are not moving. We are staying here. We had to remodel the bathroom to make it safe. And I need you to not slam any more doors because that scares me a little bit." As soon as I stopped talking, one of my son's toys downstairs suddenly played a song. And I said, "OK. I'm OK with that. That's a much more gentle response." The rest of the weekend was pretty quiet.

The poltergeist in Nora's home appeared to accept her rules—at least until she and her husband started rearranging furniture in the bedrooms. "We finally got everything moved," Nora said, "and right away I just [*pause*], I got a really bad feeling—like, he [the ghost] doesn't like this." The feeling escalated quickly. It was "a feeling in my gut that I just made a bad mistake," she said. "But I thought, 'OK. Whatever. Just get over yourself.'" Yet when she and her husband left the bedroom, the ceiling light's glass globe immediately and inexplicably fell to the ground and smashed. She again went to the basement and tried to talk to the poltergeist:

> I said, "You know, slamming doors. I asked you not to do that. And now I'm going to say don't smash lights on the floor, either—but thank you for not hitting us." And then, again, a different toy downstairs played a song. So I said, "I appreciate your response." And that was the last really noticeable thing that has happened.

About a third of all the reported ghostly encounters were what we call poltergeists. Reports of poltergeists notoriously described strange noises, objects that inexplicably moved, doors that opened and closed on their own, lights that turned on and off by themselves, and other electrical devices that operated erratically. Rarely, however, did people report seeing poltergeists—and, conversely, it was equally rare for a report of an apparition to have the characteristics of a poltergeist. Occasionally, poltergeists will damage personal property, but most reports of poltergeists described activities more akin to attention-seeking pranks.

Specters and Phantoms

We use the word "specter" to refer to any form of a menacing ghost—one by which the living feel distinctly threatened. A wraith, by definition, cannot be a specter. However, a specter can be experienced in any one of the other four ghostly forms. As discussed in Chapter 1, people typically think of ghostly encounters as a harrowing experience, but the available literature suggests the opposite (see Goldstein, Grider, and Thomas 2007; Jones 1944, 1959). This research arrives at the same conclusion. Ghosts may startle or even annoy, but they are only rarely experienced as threatening or menacing. People often use the words "freaked out" to describe their reactions to ghostly encounters, but when asked to explain the phrase, they say it is meant simply to express feelings of surprise or alarm, seldom fear. Only fourteen of the 144 reported ghosts in this study were specters (10 percent).

Ghosts are sometimes reported as playful or sad, curious or indifferent. Rarely are they angry, violent, intimidating, or aggressive. We found only two exceptions, and neither is especially frequent. The first exception was ghosts of people who had committed suicide. Amy, age nineteen, said:

> The only time I felt nauseous or, like, that I needed to get away is when my brother and his wife moved into a house, and they were giving us the whole tour. We went upstairs to these really raggedy, short stairs—they were really narrow and wooden. And I go up to this room, and [my sister-in-law] is telling me about it. I walk in and [*pause*] there was this certain spot. I was fine until I crossed the doorway, and I got this feeling like I really, really, *really* needed to get out. I couldn't breathe. I felt like someone was pressing on my chest. I said, "I don't know

about anyone else, but I really need to get out of here quick."
So we [went] downstairs, and as we [went] down the stairs, my
sister-in-law informed me that a guy hung himself on those
stairs. The realtor informed them of it.

The second exception resulted from experiences with Ouija
boards. All five reports of ghostly encounters involving Ouija boards
resulted in unpleasant experiences with specters. For example, Diane,
age twenty, agreed to try a Ouija board with her brother and friends.
"I wasn't buying it," Diane said. "[The planchette] was moving, but I
thought the boys were just screwing around, and I was, like, 'This is
stupid.'" But in the middle of the session, she recounted,

> this six-foot-four-inch star football player of the high school
> team started screaming to stop. So we stopped, turned on all
> the lights, and he was crying and hyperventilating. He said
> it felt like something, or someone, went inside him and took
> his breath from him. He felt like he had no control over his
> body. He had a severe panic attack. We stopped and didn't do
> that anymore. But we kept the Ouija board at our house for a
> while after that, and while the Ouija board was in our house,
> all kinds of really weird things happened. It didn't stop until
> we got rid of that Ouija board.

Playing with a Ouija board may be one way to anger spirits or
simply invite angry spirits to visit. Another way is to taunt and otherwise show disrespect for the dead. Our research found people who
had experienced unsolicited terrifying encounters, which I address at
the end of the chapter. However, all of the others who experienced a
reported specter—as few as they may be—associated the unpleasant
ghost with their own poor moral choices.

Josh, age twenty-three, provided the most vibrant example of this.
When he was seventeen, he and his friends visited an abandoned
cemetery with a reputation for being haunted. People around Josh's
hometown claim that the graveyard is haunted: electronic devices lose
battery power, some people have reported seeing the ghostly image
of two young girls playing ball, and others say that the names and
dates on the gravestones mysteriously change. That night, Josh and

his friends "piled into two cars," he said, and drove to the secluded cemetery, which is located in the middle of a wooded area. "Nothing really interesting happened at first," Josh recalls, but things quickly took an unexpected turn:

> I will always remember this really cocky kid that was with us— really disrespectful. He was running around the place, lying in the sunken graves and stuff, just generally being kind of a dick. We were in there for ten minutes or so before we decided to leave, just because he was really annoying us. But we had all wandered back to the farthest back part of the cemetery.

There, Josh felt a tug on his pants. "I turned around, and nothing was there," he said. "So, I mean, I can chalk things up to a little hallucination every now and then. But it just so vividly tugged that I couldn't really wave it off immediately. I got a little scared at first. Then I caught up with the group, and we started walking out." Things rapidly escalated, according to Josh:

> Another guy and I started feeling really uneasy. We turned around and both had to kind of look back at each other and confirm what we had seen. I can only describe it as a taller-than-human yet still hominid shadow with some visible eye lights of some kind. It was really indistinct in color, but you could catch the eye thing. I turned around and stayed focused forward, and my friend would look back occasionally and mention that it was getting closer—and coming out of the cemetery. He was getting a little scared, so we stopped the group for a second. That's when it got really creepy, cuz essentially it was dead silent—and no one was moving at this point—and we could hear footsteps interweaving between us, cuz there were still leaves on the ground; it was crinkling, audible, everybody heard it, and it was just [*long pause*]. Yeah, that was the point when we decided to hurry up and get out of there.

When he and his friends got back to their cars, Josh said, "the dials for my air conditioning, fan, and everything like that in my car had been changed—at least they were different from where I had left them when we got there—and all my doors were locked." They decided to leave immediately, with Josh following his friend's bright yellow car, but something was still not right:

> With the moonlight and the headlights, things would have been very visible, but the back of his car seemed almost blacked out, aside from the taillights. So the kid in my car automatically assumed it was a demon of some kind, and during the entire ten mile ride back to our city, he was, you know, praying in one way or another against it. But, I mean, we didn't make any progress with it until we got back into our town, and that's when it was even stranger because [pause] basically there is this bridge in my town, and once you get across it, you're in the main downtown part where it's really well lit. So it was still kinda blacked out on the back of his car and, um, [the kid in my car] kind of finished his prayer, at that point, and it looked almost as if the shadow fell off the back of the car and lay in the middle of the road. When I passed over the shadow, it sounded like I hit something with my car.

Simply retelling the events of that evening years later left Josh visibly shaken. Most of all, Josh was convinced that the specter that chased him and his friends from that abandoned cemetery was, in his words, "a manifestation in response to the disrespect."

Consistent with our previous distinction, a specter is encountered in a conscious state of mind. If the specter appears in, say, a dream or another altered state of awareness, we use the term "phantom." Experiences with phantoms are rare and accounted for just 6 of the 144 reported experiences with ghosts (4 percent). Julia, age twenty, for example, has experienced a reoccurring

> pattern of dreams [in which] there's something. I don't know what it is, but it's not pretty. It's like an ugly, red [pause] something. Like a red, blackish shadow. It's a patterned nightmare, where it's the same thing over and over again. At first I thought it was just a really, really scary dream—and I probably just ate something too late or whatever. But then I shared this dream with one of my roommates, and she said she's had those same

realistic nightmares, too—and one where she swears there is somebody standing in the corner of her room. Then our third roommate said the same thing—that she is having those nightmares, too. We don't want to put too much into it, but that's kinda freaky.

All of the 144 ghostly encounters reported by our respondents were experienced as an apparition, phantasm, wraith, poltergeist, specter, phantom, or some combination thereof. The most common were apparitions (45 percent) and poltergeists (32 percent), which collectively account for more than three-fourths of all reported ghostly encounters. And interestingly enough, poltergeists almost never appear as apparitions, and apparitions almost never have the characteristics of poltergeists.

THE LIMINALITY OF GHOSTS

It always happened in the basement. It's always in the basement.
—ELLA, AGE TWENTY

The concept of liminality was originally articulated to describe an ambiguous status (Turner 1969; van Gennep 1961)—when a person is between two ranks, positions, or social standings, not entirely one (anymore) or the other (yet). The concept of liminality is also frequently used to describe physical spaces that are betwixt and between. A stairway, for example, is a liminal space between one floor of a building and another. The threshold of a doorway is a liminal space; if you stand inside a doorway, you are neither in nor out of one space or the other. Liminal spaces also include window casings, hallways, basements, attics, roads, bridges, and even the space between one chapter of this book and the next.

An observant reader may already have noticed how frequently people report ghostly encounters in these liminal spaces. Examples of experiences with ghosts in liminal spaces are abundant throughout this book, and we can cite many more. For example, Dawn, age forty-eight, said that while staying overnight at a friend's home, she "was told there was a ghost in the house, but it was harmless." She was further informed that the ghost "often walked up and down the stairs, and in the upstairs hall." That evening, her son slept on the living room couch," she said. The next morning, "he asked who had been going up and down the stairs all night. There was no one that could have been walking up and down the stairs." The frequency of ghosts in liminal spaces is truly uncanny, as these examples show:

> She would see it standing in the doorway to her bedroom— and it wasn't just one time—she took a lot of comfort in its presence. Having brought it up to other members of our family, she wasn't the only one to see it, either. It was always in the doorway. (Josh, age twenty-three)

> As we were crossing the bridge, the light started flashing erratically, and the compass would spin erratically. . . . [T]hen there was a set of stairs that went down, and as we went down, his phone started going crazy again, and we saw a lot of strange blue lights. (Vicki, age nineteen)

> I looked up in my doorway, and I saw a figure. She was just standing in the door, looking at me. (Diane, age twenty)

> She was wearing the clothes she died in. She was walking down the hall and disappeared in the doorway to my room. (Gwen, age eighteen)

> I constantly see somebody in the kitchen stairwell all the time. (Grace, age forty-eight)

> I woke up, and there was a man standing in the doorway of my closet looking at me. (Jackie, age thirty-eight)

Fifty-seven of the ninety-one hauntings reported in this study (63 percent) *explicitly* described ghostly encounters that occurred in a liminal space. This is an extremely fascinating characteristic of reported ghostly encounters. After all, the ghost itself is a liminoid entity (of the living and the dead) and hence represents both an ambiguous status and a presence that frequently appears in equally betwixt and between spaces. Of course, we can offer no satisfying explanation. No one can. But the liminality of ghosts is a noteworthy characteristic that cannot be ignored.

THE (NOT SO) GENDERLESS PRESENCE

It felt like a male presence, for sure!
—CINDY, AGE TWENTY-TWO

A keen reader may have noticed something else interesting in the words people use to describe their ghostly encounters. Of the 144 reported ghosts in this study, only thirty were described as having an observable gender. Yet when people refer to ghosts, they most often use male pronouns. That is neither an accident nor a random coincidence. Presumed masculinity is not a characteristic of ghosts; instead, it is a characteristic of the people who perceive them in an androcentric culture. In contrast to the liminality of ghosts, presumed masculinity is explicable.

"I just accepted that he is here," said Nora, immediately catching herself and adding, "and I don't know why I think it's a he—but just that there is a ghost in our house." Likewise, Luke, twenty-seven, saw what "appeared to be just a dark shadow, but I took it to be a man. It just seemed like he was a guy." In three instances, people named the persistent poltergeists they experience so frequently in their homes; in each instance, the poltergeist was given a man's name. Yet characteristic of poltergeists, none were ever seen as apparitions—and none of the interviewees could explain why they thought the ghost was a man. Amy lived with a poltergeist that she and her family called "Frank." I asked Amy how she knew the presence was male—or whether she was sure of its gender at all. Amy wrinkled her forehead and replied with a puzzled look, "You know, I've never thought about that before. I dunno. My sense is that he just feels male."

Most often people tacitly presume masculinity unless a ghost is seen engaged in stereotypically feminine behavior. In other words, as a general rule, ghosts are presumed to be men unless there is evidence to the contrary. For example, Samantha, age forty-two, remembered a strange night when her son was an infant. "I was in bed," she recalled, "barely asleep and all of a sudden in my bedroom there [was] this figure. I just sensed that it [was] totally female, with dark hair, a white top, and a black bottom, but all blurry." Most important, the figure leaned over the crib where Samantha's son was sleeping "like she was going to check on him, or take care of him," she said. "When I saw that, I just freaked out. Then the woman turned and walked right through the wall." As Samantha illustrates, while she saw only a "figure," she "sensed" its gender in association with stereotypically feminine behavior.

Since 114 of the 144 reports of ghostly encounters in this study did not indicate a gender (79 percent), perhaps Jeannie Thomas (2007a: 81–82) was correct when she wrote that these ghostly encounters represent "a much greater departure from human and material reality. In the course of everyday life, how often are we in the presence of a being whose gender remains an unaddressed mystery?" Still, the tendency to *presume* masculine ghosts is not a departure from social and cultural reality at all. Instead, it is purely a product of it.

Patriarchy is about explicit and implicit power and its many manifestations in social institutions, ritual, language, customs, and ideologies that systematically privilege men over women. Waves of feminists have critiqued the historical ubiquity of male dominance and its continued manifestations in our everyday life. Androcentrism, however, is a much subtler aspect of our culture. An androcentric culture does not simply privilege masculinity. It defines masculinity in more taken-for-granted ways "as a neutral standard or norm for the culture or the species as a whole" (Lipsitz Bem 1993: 41). The tendency to regard ghosts as men in the absence of a perceptible gender is simply one of those subtle manifestations of androcentrism.

THE EVIL ONES

> The thing is, I fear rational shit—like spiders. But ghosts? Nah. I was never afraid of shit like that. I never feared it until now.
> —AARON, AGE TWENTY-THREE

As previously illustrated, people in our study seldom reported menacing experiences with ghosts. Only two of the six ghostly forms we identified—specters and phantoms—are characterized as frightening. Even combined, those were just twenty of the 144 ghosts reported (14 percent). Occasionally people reported fearsome experiences after dabbling with a Ouija board or in association with suicide deaths. In other instances, people reported chilling experiences that they perceived to be the result of their own disrespect for or outright taunting of the dead. Now and then, however, people reported profound and strikingly terrifying experiences. As Vicki, age nineteen, tried to explain:

> When we looked down at the bridge, we saw what we call "the black entity." I don't like to identify him as a ghost per se. Ghosts, for me, are more human entities—or human spirits, I guess you can say. The black entity feels a lot more dark and [*long pause*] I don't know—not human. His face was just all black. I felt threatened.

We previously cited several experiences that Grace, age forty-eight, shared with Michele and me at her home in a small rural town one cold evening in the winter of 2015. Grace has been through some tough times; her frequent ghostly encounters started occurring later in her life—"in the early [19]90s," Grace recalled—which she attributed to employment at the time that had brought her into close contact with strange people who were into strange things. "I don't even know how to put it," Grace said. "They were trying to conjure spirits and stuff. It just wasn't a good experience. . . . [T]hat's where it all came from. That's when it all started, and it never got better."

After that, Grace lived in a number of homes and apartments and reported she had experienced poltergeist activity in all of them, although some of the poltergeists were more active than others. One was entirely different. "We moved into the basement of a house, [and] it got so traumatic," she said. "We lived there for about four months before I just bolted. I broke my lease and ran. It was so freakin' scary." The haunting Grace reported experiencing there started out relatively tame—that is, the same kinds of prank-like experiences that are typical of poltergeists: "My jewelry would get moved all the time, and I'd find [it], like, hanging off a lamp finial—just in weird places like that, even on the washing machine. The washing machine and dryer would start on [their] own. The faucets would turn on; the lights would come on." Grace did not feel threatened until she started hearing a sharp voice whispering her name into her ear and could feel breath on her skin. "That's when it got *really* bad," she commented, "all in a matter of a few days." Her hands trembled as she said, "I *hate* talking about this part. I *hate* talking about that house."

After a few days of intensifying harassment, Grace experienced a specter early one morning that exhausted what remained of her tolerance. She recounted:

> I sat up out of a sound sleep. It was three o'clock in the morning on the dot; I remember looking at my alarm clock. I mean, I *sat* up and just screamed, "Holy shit!" [*showing palpable anxiety*].[9]
>
> There was a man standing in my doorway. He had on a black-and-red flannel shirt [and had] dark curly hair. I just sat there and [*pause*]. Ugh. I'm getting goosebumps just talking about it. He was a big guy, but it wasn't a guy, just standing in my doorway, looking at me. I had such catastrophic fear that [*pause*], I couldn't [*pause*]. Ugh. I couldn't move. I just closed my eyes and prayed, and prayed, and I *prayed*. When I opened my eyes again, the person, or whatever, was gone. That man [*pause*]. I [*pause*]. I don't know how to explain it other than to tell you it was just pure evil. Like a cataclysmic explosion in your head of this, this [*pause*] *fear*. I mean, it just shut me down. The only reason I can think I'd be that afraid of something is that it was just dangerous—pure evil.

"I've never been afraid like that," Grace concluded. "[The next morning], I bolted."

When asked about her religious or spiritual beliefs, Grace simply replied, "Nondenominational." She was not deeply religious, and neither were nearly all of the others who shared their ghostly experiences with us. Only four of the seventy-one participants in the study described themselves as religious. The rest used phrases such as "I grew up Catholic but don't practice it" (Hanna, age twenty-two); "I

---

9. At this point in the conversation, Grace was obviously distraught. I stopped the interview to remind her that she didn't have to answer questions if she didn't want to or talk about anything that made her uncomfortable. Grace considered taking that option but chose to finish describing what she had experienced. I express our gratitude.

was raised Christian, but I'd say I'm more spiritual than anything" (Jackie, age thirty-eight); "I'm Christian, I'd say, but I don't have a specific type of religion" (Diane, age twenty); and "I don't go to church, but I'm spiritual" (Beth, age sixty-six). Thirty-seven of the seventy-one participants (52 percent) specifically use the word "but" when asked to briefly describe their religious or spiritual beliefs; in all instances, "but" was a qualifier that distanced them from religious affiliation. This is especially significant considering that, in the few experiences reported of truly terrifying ghostly encounters, all used the word "evil," which outside religious discourse is rarely heard except as a metaphor. What these people described was not a metaphor but some kind of profound presence and a feeling of terror unlike anything they had experienced before.

Paige, age twenty-five, who described herself as "spiritual but not religious," had a series of escalating experiences over the course of five weeks that so terrified her that she described them as not only evil but also demonic. Earlier in this chapter, Paige was quoted as describing experiences of dense black shadows that moved around her bedroom. But that is not all that happened. Among the shadows, she said, "there was a presence of something evil":

I'm used to nightmares, but these were different. These were so graphic and intense. They were more violent than anything I could have ever imagined. My dreams were of self-mutilation. Me killing, like, slaughtering hundreds of people. Or me killing people that I care about. Worst of all was a sense of enjoyment in doing all that.

Paige began to see shadows and figures in her peripheral field of vision. "As time passed," she said, "I started to feel like I was in danger. I felt *literally* in danger." The shadows, apparitions, and nightmares not only persisted but also intensified. "I felt deeply oppressed," Paige said. "It was just [*pause*] evil." Exhausted and terrified, Paige finally opened up to her mother, who revealed a shocking dark secret: this wasn't the first time Paige had been harassed by the darkness. "When you were a baby," Paige's mother said to her, "you had this thing that would hover over your crib, but it had red eyes." Shocked and not quite believing, Paige asked her mother, "Why didn't you tell me this before?" to which her mother replied, "Because I didn't want to." When Paige demanded to be told, her mother reluctantly explained:

> There was this presence that would hover over your crib every night, and it had these red malicious eyes. It was a black, hooded figure, and it would come every night. Eventually, I kept you in my bed, but whatever side of the bed you were on, this thing would be on the same side. As this thing came more frequently, you started getting sick. Your skin, like, turned sickly yellowish; you started getting sores. I brought you to the doctors, but the doctors didn't know what to do. You were always crying. But every night there would be this *thing* with red eyes that would stand over you.

"I freaked out," Paige said. "My mom took me to a priest, and they performed an exorcism on me."

The vast majority of the reported ghostly encounters in our study were not threatening. Some people reported ghosts that were absolutely indifferent to the physical world and people within it. Those who provided accounts of ghosts that interacted with people were almost twice as likely to report helpful than menacing experiences. Still, on rare occasions people did report something wicked, something fearsome, and something they struggle to explain using any word other than "evil."

"MY NAME IS MADISON. THIS IS MY HOUSE."

In August 2002, Allison's family purchased a 1920 farmhouse and had it moved thirty-five miles to a small rural community. Much needed to be done to make the home "livable again," as Allison's mother recalled; a new basement had to be dug and poured, a foundation needed to be built, and the home needed wiring and plumbing. It took a month until Allison finally, and for the first time, would have a bedroom of her own.

Allison vividly recalled her excitement on move-in day: "I ran up the twelve stairs and finally reached my new bedroom." She described the "orange carpet with the brown wood-paneled walls" and said that as she unpacked, she tried to put each of her things "into the place I thought fit it perfectly." As the day waned, "I jumped onto my full-size bed—the biggest I ever had," she said. "It felt like I was sleeping on a cloud. I was feeling drowsy but had to stay up later. I started playing with my dolls." But shortly into her playtime,

> *I was sitting on the end of my bed when I heard a thud. I didn't know what to think but, being the curious little girl I was, I ran after the sound. It was coming from my bigger brothers' room. I walked across the hall. I was starting to shiver. I didn't know if I was cold or if it was something else. I hopped into their room and I looked into their closet. There was this little girl. She looked as if she was about eight. She kept telling me that daddy was mad, and she wanted me out. I didn't know what to think of the whole scenario. I just stood there. I stared at her, thinking about what to do. I was scared. Frozen. She kept repeating these two sentences: "My name is Madison. This is my house." [Then] she disappeared.*

Apparently, Allison's home was pre-occupied.

That evening, Allison said, she "couldn't fall asleep until it was almost midnight." She "kept hearing things throughout the night." The next morning, she woke up and saw words engraved in the wall that read, "My name is Madison." Allison said she "ran down the stairs faster than ever" looking for her mother, only to find her older brother consumed with a videogame. Her mother had gone out and would be home in a few hours, her brother told her. Frustrated, Allison wanted to tell her brother about her experience but said she "didn't know who to trust. . . . I needed to have my mom with me. . . . I ran back up the stairs and sat on my bed [and] before I knew it, I fell asleep. I wasn't tired, but apparently I needed rest." Her sleep was not peaceful. "I got trapped in my dream," she said. "I tried hard to wake up, but I couldn't. I opened my eyes. I was screaming, and I felt a pressure on my chest. 'My name is Madison,' I kept hearing. 'This is my house.' I was actually scared." The nightmare ended when her mother called up the stairs, "Allison, what did you need?" Allison darted out of the room and down the stairs, still crying: "'Mom,' I whispered, afraid of Madison over-hearing me, 'help me. She doesn't want us here.'"

Allison's mother, confused, said, "What are you talking about? There's nothing here." As she escorted her mother up the stairs, Allison explained that someone had written on her wall. "Just come and see," Allison insisted. But when Allison and her mother got to Allison's room and opened the door, the engravings weren't there.

For the next seven years, Allison would have regular encounters with Madison—most frequently in the large closet where she first saw her, but sometimes in the upstairs bedrooms and occasionally on the stairway between the first and second floor. Eventually, Allison regard-ed Madison as a "friend"—a word that she would later regret using to describe Madison—and said, "I do recall a lot of weird looks from my brothers when they found me 'talking to myself' in the closet."

As it turned out, Madison was a temperamental "friend"—she was prone to anger and jealousy. In their conversations, Allison said, Madison "mentioned her dad a lot and how he would be angry to see us in his home." Madison, however, seldom said much else, except to make references to other friends and family members (without naming them) and at one point making a strange request. "Madison mentioned to me about her friends having a club, and they didn't have a secret handshake—they cut each other's fingers to secure the membership as a promise that they would stay friends," Allison recounted. The ghostly girl in the closet urged Allison to join the club. "I remember refusing to take part in it because of the physical harm, and she didn't like that," Allison said. "I didn't see her for probably a week or so after that." But then, inexplicably, a deep cut about one inch long appeared on Allison's right pinky finger that was "bleeding uncontrollably." Allison said she didn't know how it happened: "I don't remember feeling it. For a cut that size, that depth, and on a finger, you would think I would remember." Madison reappeared after the injury, and to this day Allison bears the wicked scar.

Three years after the family moved into the home, Allison's little sister was born, and her brothers moved to a basement bedroom. Allison would now share a room with her sister and happily claimed her brothers' much larger former room. In the process of relocating to her new bedroom, Allison discovered a series of dated names and initials, scratched deeply and colored orange, on the inside frame of one of the house's original built-in cabinets: "Frank 1956," as well as "Tim 1965." Just below, scratched a bit more lightly and colored in red, were "Pat 1968," followed by "Kris 1977" and "Kent 1983." It seemed that every decade or so, a new youngster would call this space a bedroom, and each left a permanent record of it tucked away inside a cabinet. The oldest were the initials "V. M. E. S. 1932"—presumably the youngsters who started the tradition—only these initials were scratched not into the casing of the door but into the wainscoting itself. Ever since she discovered the initials dated 1932, Allison has openly wondered whether the letter "M" stands for

Madison and whether the other initials stand for the friends and siblings Madison spoke about but never named.

Allison's parents grew understandably concerned about, if not frustrated by, her persistent claims. When she speculated that the 1932 initials had been created by Madison, her mother snapped, "I'm sick of you trying to enforce the idea of a ghost being in my house!" and took Allison to see a therapist. The appointment didn't last long. "Mom checked us in, and I went back to the office. The therapist welcomed me, and I sat on the enormous couch, which was placed in the corner," Allison recounted. "'What are we here for today?' the therapist asked me. 'I honestly don't know,' I said. 'My mom told me I was going crazy, but she doesn't understand. Nobody does.' 'What doesn't she understand?' the therapist asked. 'Your mom told me you were here because of a little girl bothering you. Does she go to your school?' I thought for a minute, unsure about what to say. 'Not exactly,' I said. 'She lives with me.' 'Is she your sister?' the therapist asked. 'No,' I replied. 'I didn't meet her until we moved into the house.' 'How old is she?' the therapist asked. 'About eight,' I said. 'How old was she when you met her?' the therapist asked. 'Eight," I said. 'The same as now. She doesn't get older.'"

Allison remembered that the therapist "looked bewildered" and "started fumbling with her papers." She eventually stood up and said she couldn't help. The therapist discussed the brief meeting with Allison's mother, but Allison could not hear what was being said. It was the only time she was taken to a therapist.

Five years would pass, and Madison continued to visit, always appearing with "light brown hair" and dressed in clothes that, to Allison, appeared to be dated from before the 1930s. "She always smelled like perfume—'grandma's perfume,' as I called it," Allison added. "I was always cold when we were together." But while Madison did not age, she did not remain entirely unchanged over time, either. "In the beginning she appeared to me as just another person, which is why I may not have been afraid to approach her," Allison said. "Later on, she just appeared different. It's hard to explain. It's not how Hollywood portrays spirits. She wasn't see-through. But she was pale."

In contrast, Allison was growing up, changing more noticeably, and Madison was becoming more and more of a nuisance. "She started out as a friend, someone nice," Allison recalled, but "as the friendship *progressed, all that came out of it were injuries." Eventually, Allison decided to ignore the ghost that kept bothering her; without a play-mate, Madison kept to herself. But during these "quiet times," Allison said, she still heard "whispers, the closet door opening, or footsteps in the hall. Scratches would randomly appear on the paneling on my bed-room wall."*

In 2012, just before moving to a brand-new house, Allison over-heard her seven-year-old sister say into empty air, "Be quiet! You can't be talking to me when I'm around her. She might hear you." "What are you doing?" Allison asked her sister, who replied, "Nothing. Elizabeth is just being loud and annoying today. "Is Elizabeth your imaginary friend?" Allison inquired. "Yeah, kinda. She's real, though," her sister said confidently and added, "Elizabeth told me to tell you that Madi-son says hi."

Allison assured us that her sister had known nothing about her experiences with Madison:

> *That got me. I left the room [and retreated through] the door to where my bedroom once was. I sat on my bed staring at the orange carpeting. I stared at the wood-paneled walls [and pre-pared for a confrontation]. "Leave me, my sister, and my family alone!" I demanded. I sat on the bed and looked out into the hallway. I saw Madison for the first time in years. She was wear-ing the same clothes as when I met her. I walked into the hallway with my hands shaking in fear. "My name is Allison," I said with fear, "and this is my house!" Madison disappeared, and that was the last time I saw her.*

It's been three years since Allison moved from her childhood home, although her older brothers still live there. She has not had any fur-ther encounters with Madison, which helped to somewhat stem the anxiety she felt that Sunday afternoon in the spring of 2015 when she, her mother, and little sister met with Michele and me at the house. While visiting the home, Allison kept her distance from the closet and was most uncomfortable when I entered the closest myself. I made it quick and found no signs of anything unusual—not in the closet or anywhere else, for that matter. Madison appeared to be dormant. All that remained was a scar and a young woman who prefaced our ques-

tions with an understandable admission: "I must tell you that I've tried my hardest to forget the memories of this house."

What scholars call "imaginary companions" are most commonly reported among children in middle or late childhood (age six to nine and age ten to twelve, respectively) and are defined as "an invisible friend that the child talks to or plays with and refers to when communicating with others. The imaginary companion appears real to the child and the child interacts with the imaginary companion for an extended period—at least several months" (Majors 2013: 551). Scholarly research on imaginary companions is sparse, although paradoxically the available literature also reports that this is a common childhood experience. Data indicate that by age seven, 65 percent of children have had an imaginary companion (see Pearson et al. 2001; Taylor et al. 2004).

While the scholarship is thin, the few who have studied imaginary companions conclude that the experience is akin to other forms of imaginary activity in children: part of a process of developing a sophisticated symbolic concept of reality (Harris 2000), a means of acquiring coping skills (Seiffge-Krenke 1993, 1997), and part of the anticipatory socialization by which children prepare for and acquire social roles and identities (Hoff 2004–2005). Research even indicates that reported imaginary companions sometimes can be noncompliant, even unfriendly (Majors 2013). On the whole, however, children with imaginary companions report that those companions are a lot like them, share their interests, and are supportive confidants (Majors 2013).

Allison herself said she has wondered whether Madison was an imaginary friend she created. In fact, Allison preferred that conclusion because, as she put it, it seems so much "more reasonable." But for Allison, the facts don't add up, and they do not parallel what is known about imaginary companions. None of the literature reports experiences with imaginary companions that have an odor or any other kind of sensory presence. Children who report an imaginary companion refer to extended role-playing activities (Majors 2013; also see Harris 2000)—something a child does to bring about an imaginary companion in his or her mind. In contrast, according to Allison, "Madison just kind of appeared whenever she wanted to," whether she was welcome or not, and was often angry, especially as Allison grew up. Children who report imaginary companions describe interactions that *are entertaining and pleasurable, and above all, they value their imaginary friends for their support and companionship (Majors 2013). Allison's experiences with Madison were seldom enjoyable. Madison was unsupportive; she was a stubborn so-called friend who terrorized and harassed. Most significant, children who report imaginary companions know that their fictional friends are not real—they are characters of their own minds and imagination (Taylor et al. 2004)—which is quite unlike Allison's experiences with Madison. For now, Allison has simply accepted an uneasy conclusion: Madison was a ghost. The observable anxiety Allison experienced while visiting her former home that spring day in 2015 suggests she was unsure whether Madison would return; at the very least, visiting the home brought back unpleasant memories. Perhaps future research on imagined companions will discover a subset of similarly menacing imaginary "friends." But until it does, we have no evidence to argue with Allison's conclusion.*

4

GHOSTLY LEGENDS

Mary Jane Terwillegar was born on January 5, 1862, in Border Plains, Iowa.[1] She was the eighth, and last, child of John and Phoebe Terwillegar. John and Phoebe lived long lives. According to her obituary, published in the *Spirit Lake Beacon* on March 13, 1908, Phoebe was born in North Carolina in 1816 and married John Terwillegar in Illinois in 1848. John and Phoebe moved to Ohio and lived there for a little more than three years, then left for northern Iowa, where they lived for nearly twenty years. The couple's final move was to Minneota Township, on the southern border of Minnesota, where they remained as farmers until John's death on September 7, 1905, at the extraordinary age of 101. John was buried at Loon Lake Cemetery (see the image on the facing page). A compassionate obituary published in the *Spirit Lake Beacon* on September

---

1. Unless cited otherwise, the historical data for those buried in Loon Lake Cemetery come from the *Jackson County, Minnesota, Death Register* and the *Idaho County, Idaho, Death Register.* We thank Janine Porter for sharing her excellent genealogical work, which aided enormously in our reconstruction of the lives of these early pioneers.

15, 1905, refers to him as "Grandpa Twilliger [*sic*]" and states, "Peace to the spirit of a worthy pioneer."

Almost a year after John's death, Phoebe went to visit her sons in Idaho for what turned out to be an extended and final stay. Although Idaho agreed with Phoebe, who improved in health and weight, she caught a cold in February 1908 that developed into pneumonia and resulted in her death on February 26, at the almost-as-extraordinary age of ninety-two. Phoebe's remains were returned to Minnesota, where her funeral was held on March 4, followed by her burial beside her husband.

By the time John and Phoebe were interred at Loon Lake Cemetery, their youngest child, Mary Jane, had been buried in the same ground for more than twenty-five years. Unlike her parents, Mary Jane did not enjoy a long life; she died on March 5, 1880, at age seventeen. The circumstances of Mary Jane's death have been told and retold by generations of people, published in books, and propagated by the media, especially via the Internet. Hers is a tale of two accounts. First, however, we must fast forward in history a good 125 years.

Loon Lake Cemetery is currently regarded as one of the premier "paranormal hot spots" in its region. As recently as October 2012, CBS News of Minnesota listed the cemetery as one of four "best" burial grounds to visit for a "real scare from beyond the grave" (CBS News 2012). The cemetery is also identified in Mark Moran and Mark Sceurman's book *Weird U.S.*, in which one local resident is quoted as saying, "It seems like everyone in this part of the state knows about it and goes there at least once while growing up. It's given me more sleepless nights than I care to admit. I've heard too many stories and been frightened personally too many times because of it. I will never go there again" (Moran and Sceurman 2005: 297).

There are numerous apparent reasons for Loon Lake Cemetery's eerie reputation, one being its shadowy antiquity. The cemetery was established in 1876 and includes at least one hundred known interments. Some of the eternal residents of Loon Lake died before 1876, were originally buried on private property, and were relocated to the cemetery after its establishment; there are no official records for at least 10 percent of the buried (see Chonko 2013). Abandonment also contributes to its mysterious nature. The cemetery, once owned and maintained by a Methodist church, was orphaned long ago, when the church burned to the ground. No one has been buried at Loon Lake in more than ninety years. The uniqueness of the location also contributes to its eccentricity; located atop a knoll overlooking Loon Lake, the site can be seen for miles around—especially the large red pines in the center of the cemetery, which apparently were planted there, since no similar conifers are found in the groves and small stretches of deciduous trees that dot the landscape of prairie and farmland. Dishevelment further contributes to the spooky ambience. Loon Lake Cemetery is abandoned, neglected, and unkempt—virtually swallowed by overgrowth, especially ivy, prickly wild raspberry, and, above all, tall prairie grass infested with an unfathomable population of ticks. Only a fraction of the known interments in Loon Lake Cemetery are still marked by headstones; hence, considerably more human corpses lie within its earth than are identified. The road that once led to the cemetery no longer exists, and the location is primarily visited by campers from a nearby park, ghost hunters, teens seeking morbid adventures, and thrill seekers, many of whom have documented their experiences on websites devoted to the paranormal; on YouTube; and via photographs, videos, and recordings of alleged electronic voice phenomena. Yet Loon Lake Cemetery is uncanny not only, or even chiefly, because of its antiquity, abandonment, location, and abundance of unmarked graves. It is the *legend* that people tell—especially the legend of Mary Jane Terwillegar—that makes it so.

Now let us return to her story.

As the legend holds, Mary Jane Terwillegar, believed to be a witch, was beheaded in March 1880 by the citizens of nearby Petersburg, Minnesota.[2] While the legendary execution is consistent with Mary Jane's official date of death, the accounts do not specify where the alleged execution took place, although many versions claim that she is buried with the ax that severed her head. Some accounts claim that Mary Jane was not alone in her dealings with the occult—that, in fact, she was a part of a coven of witches whom the locals warily tolerated until their witchery started causing trouble "and terroriz-

---

2. Another, less often told version is that Mary Jane was discovered practicing witchcraft by her father, who buried her alive out of disgrace and fear of ridicule, and to prevent a possible lynching by his fellow townspeople.

ing the non-witch townsfolk" (quoted in Moran and Sceurman 2005: 296). Hence, in this version of the legend, two other witches were also hunted down and similarly beheaded. The witches were buried "out in Loon Lake because it was desolate and used mainly to bury orphans. In other words, these witches would be out in the middle of nowhere, not buried with the God-fearing Christians" (quoted in Moran and Sceurman 2005: 296). Indeed, people in the region often refer to Loon Lake Cemetery simply as the "witches' graveyard."

As the only witch consistently named, Mary Jane Terwillegar is the primary focus of the legend. David Ellefson, a native of the area and the original bass guitarist for the metal rock band Megadeth, grew up familiar with the legend and occasionally visited the grave. Inspired by the legend, Ellefson co-wrote the song "Mary Jane" on Megadeth's album *So Far, So Good—So What* (1989).[3] The lyrics describe being haunted by a "witch of the wind," and the words of the song's bridge section match the time- and weather-faded epitaph on her tombstone:

*Kind friends beware
as you pass by.
As you are now, so
once was I:
As I am now, so you
must be,
Prepare yourself to
follow me.*

*Although today people often find this epitaph eerie, variations of it
have been used for centuries throughout the Western world.*

These exact words constitute the epitaph on the tombstone of Clarinda Allen, who died on October 15, 1885, at age sixty-five, and was also buried at Loon Lake Cemetery. As a result, Clarinda is sometimes identified as one of Mary Jane's accomplices in the occult.

---

3. "Mary Jane" is sometimes mistakenly believed to be a song about marijuana, because the last beat of the song ends on 4:20.

These witches, and especially Mary Jane, are said to haunt Loon Lake Cemetery with a presence that can be felt: strange winds, unexplained drops in temperature, glowing orbs, and mysterious noises. It is also said that if you step on or over Mary Jane's grave, you will die an unnatural death within seventy-two hours. Local stories accentuate the threat with tales of people who have walked over the grave and come to strange and ghastly ends. An ascending fog allegedly caused one such careless visitor to pull over in his car, where he died of carbon monoxide poisoning. Local stories attribute suicides, as many as four fatal car accidents, and other tragic ends to the curse.

Yet despite all the titillating drama—witches, beheadings, strange epitaphs, a curse, and tragic deaths in what appears to be a graveyard forsaken by God and humans—what is most notable about the legend of Loon Lake Cemetery is how little of it is true, at least according to all known historical records. Mary Jane Terwillegar did die in March 1880 at the age seventeen, but she spent her final days in Cherokee, Iowa, where she worked as a domestic servant. Official records identify the cause of her death as diphtheria, a once common and deadly respiratory disease for which there was no effective immunization until the 1920s. Her remains were brought to her bereaved parents at Loon Lake, and I have no doubt that her head was fully attached to her neck.

The origins of the fabricated ghostly witch legend of Mary Jane are unclear. Mike Kirchmeier, the director of Jackson County Historical Society, is also unsure. But he has vast knowledge of the history of the area and a reasonable hunch:

> I think that story goes back to the 1880s, where there was a guy named James S. Peters who lived out there, and he had this thing about witches. In Iowa, when he ran a mill down there, things didn't go right, so he blamed it on witches. I think he brought the concept [of witches] to Jackson County and the Loon Lake area. I think that story sorta lingered just in that area with the people that lived there [until a] church [close to the cemetery] closed and they opened a bait and tackle store in there, and this guy sold beer. The neighboring county was dry, so people came from some distance to buy beer there. And so he liked the business and told the story [about the witch

cemetery down the road]. There's even an article in the paper where he bragged about it. He said, "Yeah, they liked the story, so I kinda helped it along a little bit."

Michele and I spoke with Helen, age seventy-eight, who with her husband and three children had lived and farmed on land nearly adjacent to Loon Lake Cemetery. When Helen and her husband bought the property in 1956, Loon Lake Cemetery had been abandoned for decades, and the legend was already circulating in the region. "When did you first hear of the witch legend of Loon Lake?" I asked Helen. "Oh, lord," she replied, "right after we moved there." Through the half-century that she and her husband lived on the farmstead, strangers frequently knocked on their door asking for directions to the graveyard. "People would stop by the farm all the time," Helen told us, "and at all time of the day and night. They would stop and want to know where the cemetery was. People were going out to that cemetery all the time. Toward the end, my husband got so tired of them he'd send them on a wild goose chase."

Helen's son Peter, age fifty-five, fondly remembered the cemetery. Tall enough to make seeing the bald spot on the top of his head difficult, Peter had a warm smile and a well-delivered, and equally well-intended, sarcastic wit. He enjoyed his close-knit family, frequently visiting his mother, who no longer lived at the farmstead. Peter could not decide whether to renovate the old farmhouse or put a new one on the site—or so he told us when we met him there on a warm, sunny day in the spring of 2013. He had us follow him to the now unoccupied property, the red pines of the cemetery clearly visible from his family farm.

"It's been a long time," Peter said as we walked through the tall prairie grass. "I don't remember those trees [*pointing vaguely at a small stand of relatively young hardwoods*]. After a few more long strides, he said, "That's where Jack's farmstead used to be." He pointed vaguely again, but in the opposite direction, adding, "The house was right there." His index finger pointed directly at another stand of relatively young hardwood trees. Peter recalled that Jack, the farmer who had lived there, both looked after and protected the abandoned cemetery, which would have been easy, given the close proximity of his home. Jack's former homestead had been acquired by the U.S.

Forcibly broken from its base, the headstone of Henrietta Labor lies faceup in the prairie grass. At present, the only known information about Henrietta is what is written on her vandalized headstone: born June 28, 1842; died September 28, 1901 (Chonko 2013). Beyond that, her life is a mystery, and one can only hope that in death her epitaph was fulfilled: "She passed through glories [sic] morning gate and walked in paradise."

Fish and Wildlife Services for wildlife protection, ironically leaving the cemetery defenseless.

Fascinated by the graveyard as a boy, Peter mapped the Loon Lake Cemetery and documented the names on all of its tombstones. When he was a teenager, Peter said, a newspaper reporter visited the cemetery to write a story about the witch legend. The reporter agreed to exchange a copy of the story for Peter's documentation of the graves; only Peter held up his end of that agreement, however. Still, Peter remembered the cemetery well and had no difficulty showing us the grave sites of Mary Jane, her parents, and many others he remembered—or, at least, what is left of them.

"There used to be so many," Peter commented as he peered over the graveyard with an expression as displeased as mine. Indeed, the cemetery once had at least sixty-eight headstones; when we visited in the spring of 2013, we could find only eleven (three of them newly replaced). Only one historic headstone, the farthest from the gate, is relatively intact. All of the others have been broken from their foundations, and many have been smashed into pieces that are carelessly strewn about.

The piece shown here is all that remains of the headstone of Joseph Amos. Born in France, Joseph immigrated to the United States in 1880, where he died after being thrown from his horse-drawn wagon (Chonko 2013).

The mismatched location of John Terwillegar's headstone is shown here in spring 2013. The misspelling on the headstone may have been the result of limited space, but newspaper reports and other official documents frequently used a variety of spellings for the family name.

Occasionally, headstones are placed upright on a foundation, perhaps in some small semblance of respect, but in nearly all cases they are in the wrong location and on a mismatched base. Such is the case for John Terwillegar's headstone, which we found on the opposite side of the graveyard from where it should be—perhaps just as pitiable as if it had been left where it was lying on the ground, especially considering that his headstone has been significantly damaged presumably from years of being dragged around the cemetery, and who knows where else. It also carries what appear to be two bullet holes. Most of the headstones that previously decorated Loon Lake Cemetery are missing and ostensibly have been stolen.

Police occasionally recover headstones that have been stolen from Loon Lake Cemetery. The police "find them out on people's lawns," Michael Kirchmeier told us. "They thought it was a joke. The last

Standing alone is the base stone of the marker for Harley Ralph Allen, who died young—at age twenty-one—from valvular mitral heart disease as a result of acute rheumatism. The stolen headstone, still unrecovered, is in the shape of a beautifully crafted pulpit, with a closed Bible centered at the top. Mary Chonko's (2013) comprehensive research on Loon Lake Cemetery makes excellent use of historical images to illustrate the many stunning headstones that once decorated the mostly unmarked graves.

guy [the police] caught said he took only one . . . stone. Another individual had four of them."[4] This, too, is the ultimate fate of Mary Jane Terwillegar's headstone, which was stolen in the 1990s, was recovered by the police, and is now held at the Jackson County Historical Society. After decades of abuse, including one mind-boggling incident in which, as Kirchmeier recalled, "someone had actually dug at least six feet across and down about a foot and a half trying to dig Mary Jane up," her headstone now sits on a concrete floor among a variety of other county artifacts. Perhaps as a final twist of sad irony, as of October 2013 Mary Jane's headstone is on display next to a locked

---

4. Mike also informed us that "community service" is the usual punishment these thieves get for their crimes, often to clean up the abandoned cemetery, but we saw little evidence of that.

case of Megadeth memorabilia donated to the historical society by the local rock star, including a copy of the single inspired by the legend. Only a printed photograph above Mary Jane Terwilligar's gravestone indicates where it stood before its theft.

The Jackson County Historical Society has a collection of recovered Loon Lake headstones and cannot return them to the cemetery, not only because "people won't leave them alone," as Kirchmeier rightly noted, but also because "in many cases we really don't know where the stones should be. There was never any map. We have the original plat map, but they didn't put any names in there. Through photographs and stuff we might be able to put *some* where they belong." Making the task even more difficult, a protective (but ineffectual) chain-link fence was built around the graveyard. But, Kirchmeier said, the actual cemetery "might be twice as large—the map shows a much bigger area than where they actually fenced around. Whether there are other graves farther out, I have no idea."

Loon Lake Cemetery has been destroyed—far beyond what we expected to see—and in all likelihood is unsalvageable.[5] It is a heartbreaking example of thoughtlessness, disrespect, contempt for the dead, insolence toward their living descendants, vandalism, and theft. We have been to other abandoned graveyards, and it's not unusual to see damage caused by the ravages of time, but nothing like this. It is a tragic irony that the ghostly legend of Loon Lake Cemetery warns of deadly harm that will come to those who trespass on the so-called witches' graves when, in fact, the historical truth is the exact opposite: the living have brought great harm unto the dead of Loon Lake and to their descendants.

The tragedy of Loon Lake Cemetery ought to be apparent. The large cemetery is the final resting place for the earliest pioneers who settled the region—a great many are first-wave European immigrants born in the late 1700s and early 1800s. It is also the final resting place for many who fought for rights and liberties; buried in Loon Lake are four veterans of the Civil War and one veteran of the War of 1812. Yet perhaps none feel the anger and pain over the destruction more than the descendants of those who are buried there. None of the Terwillegar family still lives in the region, and most are unaware of

---

5. The tragic destruction of Loon Lake Cemetery is an unfortunate, but excellent, illustration of why we conceal the locations of all of the allegedly haunted places we visit. Loon Lake Cemetery is the only location we chose not to conceal because, as Mike put it, "the cat is [already] out of the bag." Mary Chonko, who has worked hard to restore dignity to the cemetery, also agreed that the more people who know the truth about Loon Lake, the better. We share with many people heartfelt sadness over the irreplaceable loss of this locally important historic site.

the witch legend that surrounds their family name, as a great-great-granddaughter of John and Phoebe Terwillegar told me in a phone interview. She was unaware, she said, until she started conducting genealogical research and discovered the stories while searching the Internet to find out where Loon Lake Cemetery was located. The sadness, frustration, and anger that she expressed to me on the phone hardly require elaboration.

I have gone into great descriptive detail about the history of Loon Lake Cemetery, its ghostly witch legend, and that legend's destructive consequences. Indeed, things defined as real are real in their consequences (Thomas and Thomas 1928). There are no witches in Loon Lake Cemetery, any more than there were witches in Salem village in 1692. Yet what was defined as witchery resulted in the real execution of nineteen people in 1692, just as the ghostly witch legend of Loon Lake Cemetery has been instrumental in its destruction. Description, however, is just one of three primary objectives of any social or cultural analysis. We must also render some kind of explanation and some measure of understanding. In this case, the proverbial devil is once again in the details.

Places of abandonment are easy targets for vandalism, as a few accounts of ghostly encounters cited in earlier chapters have illustrated. Likewise, some of our informants recalled adolescent thrill seeking that involved trips to graveyards and engaging in behavior that may be seen as disrespectful. But none involved vandalizing gravesites, malicious destruction, or theft. In the course of this research, we visited several abandoned graveyards about which spooky stories are told, but nowhere else did we see evidence of intentional wreckage.

For comparison, consider Framton Cemetery,[6] located about one hundred miles from Loon Lake. Framton Cemetery is also abandoned; it is all that remains of a small but once vibrant community primarily occupied between 1869 and 1878. Framton had a general store, a post office, a sawmill, and a blacksmith's shop, but when it was bypassed by railroads, it was economically choked into extinction, even as a neighboring community twelve miles south enjoyed a boom brought by people and goods the rails delivered. Framton is

---

6. "Framton Cemetery" is a pseudonym.

a ghost town, and fittingly, the cemetery is the last surviving major artifact of its existence.

Framton Cemetery is not only abandoned like Loon Lake but also located in an obscure rural location.[7] In fact, Framton Cemetery is now completely shrouded by the thick surrounding forest. Consequently, it is even less visible to the public eye than Loon Lake. Deviant activities can easily occur at Framton Cemetery with little fear of unwanted eyes watching.

Like Loon Lake, people claim to have ghostly experiences in Framton Cemetery and, frankly, the location is much creepier. A narrow, winding path through the forest leads to the cemetery gate, which zigzags visitors in a bizarre "Z" formation. Inside the cemetery there appears to be little semblance of order to the gravesites. Most of the dead were buried in pine caskets that have long since rotted, with the earth above sinking and collapsing on the corpse, resulting in unnerving sunken graves. Most unusual of all, at the back of the cemetery is an elaborate marble headstone for twin girls who died in May 1876. Their gravestone is fenced in and set apart from the surrounding graves, and it is not surprising that most of the eerie stories that the locals tell about Framton Cemetery concern this oddity. So like Loon Lake, Framton Cemetery has a gravesite and headstone that attracts curiosity and attention and serves as an anchor for ghostly encounters and the stories that people tell about them.

Yet nowhere in Framton is there evidence of vandalism and theft. Some headstones have been upheaved but only because a tree has sprouted and grown and bullied the dead and his or her marker aside. Some headstones are broken, but only because of the region's climate, where the freezing and thawing of water easily cracks the hardest stones. Most of these headstones have seen more than 140 winters. Most revealing of all is how visitors to Framton Cemetery have interacted with the broken headstones over time: in all cases, they have been reassembled, like jigsaw puzzles, in their proper locations, with few, if any, missing pieces:

---

7. Locations like these are often well known to local residents but exceedingly difficult for outsiders to find. In our fieldwork, we frequently needed extremely detailed directions or, even better, a gracious local guide just to find them.

And when possible, the broken parts of the headstones at Framton Cemetery are returned to their proper upright placement, as was the standard government-issue Civil War veteran's headstone of Jno Okins. Why, then, is Loon Lake Cemetery subjected to such destruction when cemeteries such as Framton have all of the same qualities? Why have people shown the dead of Framton respect over the course of many decades that has not been accorded to the deceased of Loon Lake? The answer, I believe, lies entirely in the ghostly witch legend. Ghosts may haunt Framton Cemetery and places like it, and I have spoken to many people who are sure that is true. But the ghosts of Framton, unlike those of Loon Lake, are the ghosts of *people.*

Ordinary everyday people are capable of committing atrocious acts, something Philip Zimbardo (2007) fittingly refers to as "the Lucifer effect." Adolf Hitler could not have accomplished his objectives had it not been for the willing participation of millions of everyday people who were not unlike you and me. The same can be said for any number of countless acts of genocide, mass murder, barbarism, colonization, enslavement, expulsion of people, and so on. *Dehumanization* is central to the process by which otherwise good people can do very bad things to others. Once targeted individuals or popula-

tions are stripped of their humanity—whether they are Jews, Native Americans, blacks, gays, or, in this case, "witches"—human rights and dignities are potentially forfeit. Such people may even be seen as a threat to cherished beliefs and values and thus deserving of punishment, torment, and exploitation—perhaps even requiring expulsion or execution. In short, it is easier to enslave, torture, humiliate, or kill a beast or monster than a person. History is riddled with examples of the unfortunate process of dehumanization that characteristically triggers the Lucifer effect, to tragic ends. Decades of social science research has illustrated how even subtle aspects of a situation can bring about this bad quality in people.

The legend of Loon Lake Cemetery unambiguously describes the beheading of people for the crime of witchcraft and, by default, the justness of the executions. Implicit in the legend is that witches are undeserving of their human right to life. That does not only happen in legend. It happened in Salem, Massachusetts, in 1692 and for centuries in Europe before that. It is still happening in Papua New Guinea, where women branded as witches are stripped naked before lynch mobs that blindfold them, slash them with knives, and burn them alive for all to see. The human rights and dignities that are denied to living witches, in this case, can linger long after death. The destruction of Loon Lake Cemetery is one such manifestation. Framton Cemetery may be haunted by ghosts of people, but Loon Lake has the ghosts of *witches*. Hence, the respect people have shown toward the former residents of Framton is conspicuously absent in the "witches' graveyard," and this, no doubt, is a major part of the reason people commit acts at Loon Lake Cemetery that they otherwise would find morally objectionable.

The conclusion is clear: the legend surrounding Mary Jane Terwillegar and the cemetery in which she is buried is not true, yet witches *do* haunt Loon Lake—active, potent, destructive, and immoral witches. The source of their power lies not in magic or sorcery but in the minds, words, and actions of the people who come calling. Indeed, as Stephan Asma (2009: 14) wrote, "If we find monsters in our world, it is sometimes because they are really there and sometimes because we have brought them with us."

The previous chapters of this book concern firsthand accounts of ghostly encounters, or what folklorists more accurately call "memorates"—that is, narratives that are fashioned from memory and convey personal experience. Folklore is different. Folklore refers to the legends, myths, and tall tales that people tell as part of the tradition of a given culture, subculture, group of people or, as the legend of Loon Lake Cemetery illustrates, region where people reside. Ghostly legends are told by people, and as several people reported in this study, those stories may compel them to visit these places said to be haunted. But rarely do those visits result in uncanny experiences. The young woman who introduced Michele and me to the legend of Loon Lake Cemetery grew up in the region; she also accompanied us during our fieldwork. She would not, however, enter the cemetery. "I will not go in there. That place just gives me the creeps," she said, although she had never experienced anything strange or bizarre at Loon Lake (or anywhere else, for that matter). Still, she grew up hearing the legend, and the story alone was enough to frighten her. In this way, ghostly legends "contain spirits; they capture them" in a *narrative* form, not an experiential one (Goldstein, Grider, and Thomas 2007: 2).

Folklorists have contributed greatly to our understanding of ghostly legends, and they are the only scholars to have amassed a significant body of research on ghosts. The most comprehensive, contemporary, and impressive is *Haunting Experiences* (2007), by Diane Goldstein, Sylvia Grider, and Jeannie Thomas, which unpacks the significance of ghost lore in the context of commodification, popular culture, and mass media. Barbara Walker's edited collection *Out of the Ordinary* (1995) is equally impressive, although not entirely focused on ghost lore. The vast majority of other works by folklorists, not unlike this research, focus on ghost lore of a specific region or population of people. Gillian Bennett's *Alas, Poor Ghost!* (1999) is a sophisticated analysis of ghost lore among elderly women in England. Elizabeth Tucker's *Haunted Halls* (2007) examines the role and functions of ghost lore on American college campuses. Louis Jones examined the ghost lore of New York in his classic *Things That Go Bump in the Night* (1959), and Judith Richardson's *Possessions* (2003) focuses exclusively on ghost stories of the Hudson Valley. Yet regardless of their differences, folklorists, each in their own way, illustrate the various and complex intersections of ghost lore and culture.

In this chapter, we have chosen to focus on one ghostly legend to illustrate in detail how the stories that people tell are not only a product and reflection of culture. Certainly, folklorists are correct to emphasize the ways that ghost lore is made meaningful in cultural milieus, which explains and justifies why folklorists mostly focus on the ghost lore of specific regions or groups of people. But there is more. *Stories also motivate action.* Regardless of the truth, the content of the tales that people tell make some actions more likely than others.

GHOSTLY GENESIS

Twenty-seven-year-old Tara bought her house in February 2011. It is a very large house in a very small rural town. The grandness of the home, a Victorian that dates to 1863, has been diminished a little by exterior and interior renovations over the years; the past five decades, in particular, have left the home a tattered mixture of dated aesthetics from 1960s, 1970s, and 1980s. But it has "good bones," as they say: the roof and foundation are solid, the characteristic exterior features are intact, the hardwood floors simply need refinishing, and the crown molding and oak trim work are all original. Tara knows the home needs some tender loving care and has already made excellent progress toward restoring it to showcase its intrinsic grandeur. This kind of do-it-yourself renovation is daunting and requires committed labor over the course of many years. But as a former Marine who survived multiple combat deployments, Tara knows more about determination and resilience than the average homeowner.

Tara experiences a variety of uncanny events in her home. For example, one night while she was reading in bed, with her boyfriend at the time sleeping next to her and the television on for background noise, "the TV just went off," she said. "I tried to turn it back on with the remote, but it wouldn't turn on. So I got up to turn it on, and it wouldn't. I thought that maybe something had shorted. So I started reading again, and then I heard voices downstairs in the living room and started freaking out. I pushed [my boyfriend] to get him to wake up cuz I wanted him to check it out. [He] mumbled a bit and got out of bed as the voices started getting louder."

Tara's boyfriend cautiously descended the two flights of oak stairs. "He made it about halfway down the stairs [before realizing that] the TV in the living room somehow got turned on," with the volume increasing incrementally, Tara said. "By the time he made it to the bottom of the stairs, it was all the way up—the volume was all the way." He "turned off the TV, crawled into bed, and just lay there for a while with his eyes open." They both remained unsettled and unsure of what had happened. "I don't know how the TV got turned on, [not to mention] why the volume kept turning up," Tara said. "It was just really creepy."

Tara's dining room walls feature large canvas oil paintings that she adores. "They get tilted all the time," Tara said. "One gets more askew than the others. C'mon, let me show you." Tara stood up from her living room couch in what would originally have been a parlor. We followed her into the dining room as she pointed to a large, tastefully painted nude feminine figure. "Like that," Tara said as she tilted the picture several inches clockwise. "I know that just walking in the room creates vibrations that can tilt a picture on the wall—but not like that! And I used to have this painting on that wall [pointing across the room], where it did the same thing. That's why I moved it, but it still does this." Tara continued, "And that's the other thing—it happens so dramatically. I'll walk through the dining room into the kitchen to get something to drink. The painting will be straight when I first walk by, but when I return a few minutes later, it's tilted like this. It's just enough to drive me bonkers."[1]

Several months after our first visit to her home, Tara got in touch with me. Something new was happening. Tara has a cabinet in which she displays, as she said, "knick-knacks and crap my family gives me," including four porcelain cherubs. "I've been coming home lately to those cherubs—two in particular—that have somehow gotten out of the cabinet on their own," Tara explained. "It happened three times in the last two weeks." Even more perplexing to Tara are the peculiar places where she consistently finds the wandering cherubs:

> The one cherub that lies down, with his head in his hands, is usually on top of my washer or dryer. The other cherub that's kneeling is usually beside my computer. There are four cherubs in the cabinet, but only those two somehow get out of the cabinet on their own. I mean, I live alone now. I've changed out the locks, and I'm the only one who has keys to my house.

Tara described these and other minor annoyances—frequent uncanny happenings that are highly characteristic of a poltergeist. "It's

---

1. Four months later, Tara, frustrated but determined, rehung the artwork on two nails about six inches apart. That should have solved the problem, but it didn't. The painting continues to tilt just as much as before. "It's really starting to piss me off," Tara said.

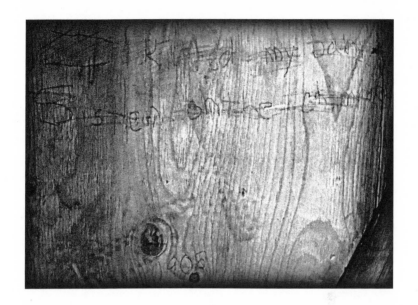

just kind of awkward, and sometimes annoying," she said. "I'm not afraid or anything like that." But there is one exception to Tara's experience. There is something unique about Tara's home and the poltergeist that presumably shares residence, something that is even more strange and unsettling than the various mysterious happenings Tara describes, something that Tara discovered in the home.

When Tara purchased the home, the previous owners had left behind what she described as "a bunch of junk in the attic." When she finally got around to cleaning the area out, Tara noticed something she had not seen before: a confession scratched into a board on the roof decking behind the chimney. It read, "I killed my baby sister on the chimney," and was dated 1905. The murder confession helps Tara make uneasy sense of the many strange things that occur in the home. Unlike nearly all of the others we spoke to, Tara found a possible clue to help explain why she experiences a ghostly presence.

Only about half of the ghostly encounters in this study involve an apparition of any kind, so ghosts are just as likely to have an invisible presence as they are to be seen. Even when apparitions are reported, 32 percent are not in an observable human form. Thus, the majority of ghosts reported in this study are nameless, faceless, genderless, age-

less, and raceless and are only presumed to be former living people.[2]
*Moreover, ghosts seldom vocalize, and even when they do speak, they
rarely say more than a single word or phrase. Only three participants
in this study reported having had a genuine conversation with a ghost,
and in each instance the ghosts were reluctant to divulge information.
Sixteen-year-old Allison spent most of her childhood interacting with a
ghost who called herself Madison and whom Allison frequently saw in a
closet. Over time, Allison got a fair amount of information from Madison, who insisted, "This is my house" and referred to her angry father,
her siblings, friends, and a strange friendship initiation ritual but had
nothing to say about anything else. Twenty-year-old Maggie described a
similar experience. She, too, vividly recalled frequent interactions with
a ghost in her bedroom closet, a little boy who "would always tell me,
'My name is Quimby.'" Maggie specifically remembered asking questions but getting little, if any, response. Thus, even the most intelligent
of the "intelligent hauntings" reported in this study did not entail spirits
that were willing to disclose much information, if any at all.*

*The reported experiences in this study are overwhelmingly devoid
of clues to why the ghost is haunting. Since ghosts are unwilling to
explain themselves, people are left to their own limited resources to
find answers. As Nora said about the poltergeist in her 1970s rambler-
style home:*

> *I have curiosity, but I don't know why he is here. I have no idea.
> I don't know if this used to be his house or what. The curiosity,
> at this point, makes me want to find answers. I mean, I've got
> the paperwork for the house, and that will give me information
> about past owners. But I don't know if that would even answer
> my questions. I don't know.*

*In sixty of the ninety-one reported hauntings in this study (66 per-
cent), informants had no explanation for the ghostly encounters they*

---

2. Although this is not always true. Three people reported having had a ghostly
encounter with a deceased pet. Another informant reported typical poltergeist
activity that included objects tipping over and sometimes being flung across the
floor; that informant concluded that she lived with the ghost of a cat, because
these were actions she associated with indoor felines.

reported. Only thirty-one reported hauntings, roughly a third, offered an even loosely assembled explanation for the ghosts being reported. The few participants in the study who had an explanation, regardless of how thin, universally reported one of two justifications for why the ghost was haunting. Some reported ambiguous hunches about deceased relatives or former residents of their homes; others relied on rumors of murder, suicide, or fatal accidents.

Heidi and her live-in boyfriend reported hearing mysterious voices and one incident in which they both saw an apparition, but neither was able to hear or see any distinguishing characteristics. "We don't know who or what it could possibly be," Heidi said. "If anything, it's, like, a dead grandparent or something. But we have no clue." Other informants simply assumed the ghost was a departed former resident of the home. As thirty-eight-year-old Tiffany explained, "We just thought it had to be Randy, because that's the only thing that made sense, since he built the house and he died there."

In contrast to the informants who made vague guesses about deceased relatives and former residents of their homes, others in the study explained the genesis of ghosts by citing stories about murder, suicide, and fatal accidents. Twenty-eight-year-old Sarah recalled that when she was in sixth grade, she moved from "a very comfortable childhood home to this huge, disgusting building." Sarah never felt comfortable in the new home and experienced a variety of uncanny happenings that are characteristic of a poltergeist. "Right at the window where I slept, someone got pushed off the roof there and died," she told us. "My bedroom shared a window right where the guy died—where he was murdered."

Likewise, suicides are presumed to generate ghosts, although suicidal ghosts were reported even more tentatively than were the alleged murders. "Apparently, one of the previous owners tried to kill himself; he shot himself in the stomach but didn't [immediately] succeed," said twenty-seven-year-old Luke while talking about the poltergeist he and his girlfriend had experienced. "He went to the hospital, lived for a little while, but died not long after. I don't know if that would explain it or not."

Finally, when people search for answers for why ghosts haunt, any rumored story of a fatal accident in the vicinity is fair game—although as in the instances of alleged murders and suicides, none of these stories *could be verified. For years, Hannah, a twenty-two-year-old nursing assistant, her co-workers, and residents of the nursing home where she worked reported seeing a little boy wearing overalls "at least once every couple months." His presence was simply attributed to a rumored fatal accident in the vicinity, as Hannah described:*

> *People say that it is because a little boy drowned in the ravine next to the nursing home. The nursing home is kind of secluded back in the woods. So they say that the little boy drowned back there. But I don't know how true that is. That's the story the employees say, but I don't know what their sources are or if it is true. It's just accepted.*

From what and why are ghosts believed to haunt? Most of the informants in this study did not have a clue, let alone an answer. Those who had a conjecture relied on vague associations—ambiguous correlations that were broad enough conceivably to account for uncanny experiences that could happen to anyone and anywhere. Even those who had discovered clues could not be certain. Tara admittedly did not know whether the murder confession scratched into an old board in her attic was related to the poltergeist she reportedly experienced, but from her point of view, "It seem[ed] like it could be legit" (emphasis added).

Folklorists who have studied ghost lore have discovered patterns in the genesis of ghosts that reflect social and cultural realities. In her study of ghost lore on American college campuses, Elizabeth Tucker (2005: 191) found tales that "often emphasize drugs, aberrant behavior, and a propensity for occult activities, as well as suicide," that function as precautionary warnings for living students at those colleges and universities. Louis Jones's (1944: 244) study of ghost lore in New York found that "more than a third of our ghosts died violent or sudden deaths. The largest number of these were murdered, and while the murderers seldom return, the victims of murder seem particularly restless."

Jeannie Thomas (2007a: 41) analyzed folklore of ghosts that return to repay debts, emphasizing how the stories reinforce "the cultural value that debts should be paid." Thomas (2007b: 81) also found that "wronged parties of either gender are among the most common types of ghosts" and ghostly folklore both reflects and reinforces traditional gender roles.

In our study, however, two-thirds of the participants had no explanation at all for why the ghosts they reported experiencing are haunting. For the majority of people who report a ghostly encounter, "No explanations or analysis are ever offered—only stories" (Clarke 2012: 179). Those who do offer an explanation rely on vague and speculative hunches. None of those speculative hunches explicitly states a motive for why ghosts are haunting. But that is not surprising. Folklorists study the stories that people tell, and most stories, even simple ones, have a plot with the basic requisites of exposition: rising action, climax, falling action, and resolution. In contrast, our study focuses on the experiences that people report, and while many are dramatic, only rarely do they have a plot.

5

GHOSTLY SPECULATIONS

> Ghosts remain with us in all these venues because they give voice to both the everyday and the extraordinary experiences that haunt us.
>
> —Diane Goldstein, Sylvia Grider, and Jeannie Thomas, *Haunting Experiences*

Michele and I concluded our fieldwork on a sunny, humid afternoon in May 2015 with a visit to the fifteenth haunted house in this study. We enjoyed all of our fieldwork and have fond memories of the people and places we visited, but it is a special privilege to be welcomed into someone's home. Michele and I listen carefully to what people say, ask a lot of questions, see for ourselves these places that ghosts are said to haunt and, if given permission, record and photograph what we hear and observe. Fieldwork is about gathering as much information as possible. Once we express our gratitude and say goodbye, the analysis begins as Michele and I drive home, sharing our observations and thoughts.

It's a good thing we didn't have to travel far for our last site visit. A thunderstorm was rapidly approaching on the western horizon, and we had left windows open at our house. I risked a little more speed than usual on the drive home. We had exhausted our immediate observations and thoughts on what we had just seen and heard, and Michele changed the topic. "You know," she said to me, "when we visit these places, just once I'd like to experience something unusual."

For two years we met with a lot of people who reported ghostly encounters. We spent a lot of time in basements, attics, and graveyards. My research reimbursement forms showed a total of 5,208 travel miles for the study, and we had seen much. We took hundreds of pictures. None of our photos contained anything uncanny—not even one strange orb or inexplicable mist. Some were out of focus (my fault), and a couple had large black shadows in the upper right corner of the frame (which I'm sure is my finger). We recorded more than twelve hours of interview data; none of the recordings contain electronic voice phenomena or anything else inexplicable. Michele was right. Although we had seen a lot and conversed with plenty of people who spoke about things they could not rationally explain, we did not experience anything unusual for ourselves in our fieldwork. Still one thing was for certain: we saw many ghosts. We just had to discover where to look for them.

When people think of ghosts, the common attitude seems to be to relegate the experiences to something akin to fart jokes and campfire stories—amusing and entertaining but on the whole inconsequential, easily dismissed, and inappropriate for serious audiences. We encountered little of that. In fact, early in the data collection I learned to include tissues in my ethnography field kit because the experiences people share were sometimes filled with tears of gut-wrenching grief. I should have anticipated this. Ghosts are presumed to be visitations by dead people, some of whom have left behind loved ones who miss them terribly. All of those experiences touched my heart, but none did so more than that of Riley. Earlier in this book, I wrote that I "saw an undeniable ghost in Riley's eyes" when tears streamed down her cheek as she struggled to explain how the ghost of her beloved sister—torn from her life by a tragic accident—continued to have a presence in her life. Riley's experiences now haunt me, too and, while the image of her tearful face is burned into my mind's eye, I struggle to understand how anyone else can fail to see that ghost as clearly as I do.

Ghost hunters and supernatural thrill seekers flock to Loon Lake Cemetery in search of a ghostly encounter at a presumed witch's grave. Some claim to have had eerie experiences at Loon Lake, and some have even documented those experiences in photographs, videos, and electronic audio recordings. In our visits, we did not experience anything unusual at Loon Lake. Nonetheless, we saw ghosts scattered all around the cemetery. They were most immediately apparent in each stolen, shattered, or vandalized headstone. We saw those ghosts again when we visited the Jackson County Historical Society and observed recovered stolen headstones displayed next to a collection of Megadeth memorabilia. Once again, I struggle to understand how others cannot see those ghosts.

I encountered Brian again seventeen months after our interview in his parents' basement. "Nah, I haven't done that in a long time," Brian said when I asked him about his formerly frequent visits to abandoned homes and haunted cemeteries. Brian hasn't lost interest; he just doesn't have the time anymore. Shortly after our interview in November 2013, Brian found a girlfriend. A few months later, they were living together, and ten months after that, they became parents. Brian has maintained his job as a low-level fast-food employee, and that provided enough money for him to buy a used car. His teenage girlfriend is unemployed, however, and the young couple struggle to make ends meet. All that remains of Brian's former self is a ghost that haunts liminal pages of this book.

Previous pages also include Karen's account of her and her family watching her grandmother pass away in a hospital bed. Karen described the experience as "traumatizing" but felt comforted when the wraith of her grandmother touched her shoulder and appeared to her and her family. Karen reported seeing a ghostly image of her grandmother, yet at that moment the reverse also became true. Inside Karen is the genetic imprint of all her relatives; Karen is now the living ghost of her deceased grandmother. So are we all. "The DNA each of us carries in our bodies makes us all ghosts," Jeannie Thomas (2007a: 25) insightfully writes; our "DNA makes us, in part, the ghosts of our ancestors. We embody scraps, fragments, and glimmers of our forebears. We are shadows of who they were."

In one respect, a ghost is nothing more or less than a lingering presence. That lingering presence may be comforting or terrifying, beneficial or destructive, puzzling or predictable. But one thing is certain: ghosts are unavoidably all around us and are often taken quite seriously. For example, in my professional life as a sociologist of the symbolic interactionist tradition, I frequently encounter the ghosts of George Herbert Mead, Charles Horton Cooley, Herbert Blumer, Erving Goffman, and many others. Sometimes the ghosts of Karl Marx and Max Weber visit me, but my colleagues down the hall see them far more often than I do. Regardless of intellectual influences, one may even argue that reading this book is a ghostly encounter: "like ghosts, words are disembodied presences" (Bergland 2000: 5) and have the power to communicate without the physical presence of the author and from beyond the grave. The lingering presence of ghosts surrounds us, because, as Avery Gordon (1997: 23) writes, "Ghostly matters are part of social life."

Shortly before we concluded our fieldwork, a colleague asked about our research. I shared with him some of the most recent work we had done, and he listened with both interest and amusement. In our fieldwork, Michele and I listened more than we spoke to people, but inevitably we had a lot of questions. When people ask about the research, it is always the other way around: we talk while others listen. There is another difference, too. When people ask about our ghost research, they seldom have many questions. In fact, my colleague had just one. "Dennis," he said, "you don't actually believe these people, do you?" I can hardly blame him for asking. A few years earlier, I might have asked the same question myself. I don't anymore.

GHOSTLY ONTOLOGY

> It has never been easier to be a skeptic, which is not necessarily good for skepticism.
> —PETER LAMONT, *EXTRAORDINARY BELIEFS*

The question my colleague asked is one I encounter frequently. How I answer it isn't irrelevant, but I would like to suggest that my answer is less significant than the presence and persistence of the question. I've made a career out of studying a lot of strange and unusual things that other sociologists haven't studied, wouldn't study, or perhaps didn't think of studying: nudity and nakedness (Waskul 2002), the social and cultural significance of smell and odor (Waskul and Vannini 2008), going to the bathroom (Waskul 2015), the processes by which women discover their clitoris (Waskul, Vannini, and Wiesen 2007), and lying and deceitfulness (Waskul 2009), just to name a few. I'm accustomed to seeing puzzled expressions when colleagues hear my answers to their question "What are you studying *now*?" It's a question I honestly don't mind answering. Although my research topic might not have occurred to them, they usually understand its social and cultural significance once they've heard my explanation. To question why something is *relevant* is customary and should be expected, but that is not the same as questioning whether something is *real*. Never before have I confronted that question, and with such frequency.

Scholars in the social sciences are exceptionally skilled at epistemological relativity—that is, we understand that truth is a matter of perspective, highly subject to frameworks of interpretation, history, language, and other symbolic dimensions of culture. In fact, a great deal of theory and research in the social sciences is precisely intended to understand those processes. A good argument can be made for epistemological relativity as the bedrock of the social sciences. In my discipline, students of sociology can earn brownie points simply by raising their hands in class and asking, "Isn't gender [or race, age, time, selfhood, sexual orientation, emotions, or any other topic under discussion] just a social construction?" The bedrock assumption in sociology isn't *whether* things are socially constructed but *how* and to what *consequence* (positive or negative, explicit or covert). This is epistemological relativity at its finest.

Can the same be said for ontological relativity? Some might argue that epistemological relativity and ontological relativity are one and the same. For example, the processes by which gender is socially constructed are precisely what make masculinity, femininity, and other constructions of gender real for people. A few years ago I might have made this argument myself. But to what extent is that convenient answer simply a product of having shifted our confidence in what is real? As noted earlier, I am a sociologist of the symbolic interactionist tradition; the actions people take toward things and the emergent meanings things have for them are the starting point for all analysis. *That* is what I've been trained to accept as real and subsequently scrutinize with empirical research. I've done that in the pages of this book, most explicitly in Chapter 2, by examining the processes by which uncanny happenings are made into ghosts. I'm going to do it at least one more time before the book ends. But it's important to note that such an analysis builds from *ontological certainty*, not relativity.

From the onset of this study, I sought to maintain epistemological relativity and at least *some* degree of ontological relativity. After all, how could I possibly seek to understand something I've already dismissed as unreal? Still, I have to admit that in terms of ontological relativity, this study is at least a partial failure. In fact, I've come to conclude that scholars are *too* certain about what is real. Perhaps that is as unavoidable as it is inevitable if we are to conduct analysis at all. But to answer my colleague's question: of course I believe what people have reported in this study. I understand that when we talk to, interview, and survey people, they *may* exaggerate, they *may* present themselves in a manner intended to be flattering, and memory isn't always accurate. But none of that makes the things that people say untrue, and how people report things is just as important as the content of what they say. Sigmund Freud stated it well in *The Uncanny*:

> We know now that what we are presented with are not figments of a madman's imagination, behind which we, with our superior rationality, can recognize the sober truth—yet this clear knowledge in no way diminishes the impression of the uncanny [and] in no way helps us to understand this uncanny effect. (Freud 2003 [1919]: 139)

I would simply add a fundamental truism from my end of the social sciences—once defined as real, things are real in their consequences—and that goes a long way toward understanding "this uncanny effect."

GHOSTLY AMBIENCES

> An uncanny effect often arises when the boundary between fantasy and reality is blurred, when we are faced with the reality of something that we have until now considered imaginary.
> —SIGMUND FREUD, *THE UNCANNY*

None of the ghosts Michele and I saw with the people we spoke to and in the places we visited were a literal presence of a formerly living person. More precisely, all of the various "lingering presences" were made evident to us in the *things that people did* in response to what they defined as a ghostly encounter. Thus, I admittedly have dodged the main questions most people have about uncanny experiences. In fact, I have sidestepped that issue throughout the book, perhaps frustrating readers who are searching for a voice of authority to confirm the existence of ghosts, as well as the skeptics who expect the opposite from someone who calls himself a scholar. To be clear, I have deliberately evaded the issue because, regardless of whether ghosts exist, the things that people do in response to uncanny experiences are undeniably real and have consequences of their own. We hope the pages of this book have made that abundantly clear. But, now, let's address the issue directly. What exactly did these people experience?

I cannot say with any certainty that the people we spoke to had experienced a ghostly presence, and equally I cannot say they had not. I can report that there is no evidence to indicate that the participants in this study were fabricating or embellishing. In fact, the evidence shows the opposite. The people I spoke to were keenly aware of how irrational their stories sounded. Seventeen times people said, "I know this sounds crazy" or "You're going to think I'm crazy" or made some other statement intended to convey that they were sane enough to acknowledge how bizarre their experiences sounded. Most wouldn't even speak to Michele or me until they felt sure that we were not interested in discrediting or ridiculing the experiences they were reporting. In the course of this research, I was approached by four potential participants who chose not to share their experiences because nothing I said about confidentiality or my sympathetic ear made them feel comfortable enough to do so. I often observed considerable anxiety in the voices and body language of many people we spoke to; whatever it is they experienced, it certainly left an imprint. Ultimately, however, it is impossible to know what it is that these people have experienced.

But now, and with significant trepidation, I must keep a promise I made in June 2013: "I will tell the truth." It is true, and Michele is right—we did not experience anything uncanny in our fieldwork. However, that admission is true only because it includes the word "fieldwork"; we did not experience anything unusual in the places we visited or among the people we spoke to. That said, in the course of this research I did, in fact, experience *a lot* of uncanny ambiences and inexplicable happenings, and they occurred frequently enough to cause me to doubt at times whether if I could carry on with the research at all.

I never experienced anything I thought might be a ghostly presence before we started data collection. That changed quickly and almost immediately. When, eighteen months into our data collection, Aaron, age twenty-three, said, "I thought it was just my eyes playing tricks on me—and the majority of it could be, and probably is," about three shadows that had followed him for days, I nodded my head in agreement because I knew *exactly* what he was talking about.

Scholars speak and write a lot about why they study the things they do, how they conduct their research, what they found, and what it all means. Scholars sometimes report what their research does for them. But scholars seldom talk or write about what their research does *to* them. I don't recall ever having that conversation, and I'm unaware of published literature on the topic. When I conduct research, the task utterly possesses me. That happens during every study I conduct, and this one was no exception. And the result of what that possession did *to* me was not at all pleasant.

When I wasn't reading about ghosts, I was talking to someone about them; visiting a place said to be haunted; transcribing or writing field notes; coding data, exploring themes that emerged from what people said, and drawing parallels and contrasts; or writing and revising endless drafts of what would become the chapters of this book. I was also persistently thinking about ghostly experiences—often crafting sentences in my head and writing them down on scraps of paper for later reference. The thinking part is especially possessive; the research is on my mind all the time, and I have found that long drives and meetings (especially boring meetings) are ideal times to craft lengthier sets of ideas in my head.

For two years I was possessed in mind and body by ghosts and ghostly experiences. The combination of constant preoccupation and large blocks of intense thought became a recipe for unsettling experiences. I, like Aaron, am certain most of it was a product of my own mind and frayed nerves. Countless times I was startled by our stealthy cat, something I never experienced before this study. Countless times I was distracted by the kind of strange shadow or peculiar noise that I'm sure I experienced but didn't pay particular attention or assign meaning to before conducting the study. I dream vividly, sometimes lucidly, and in color. I won't bother commenting on lost sleep. I get especially jumpy after long blocks of writing or analysis, and in those moments even ordinary inanimate objects in my environment have the power to startle me. For example, during one period of writer's block, I left my second-floor home office to start a load of laundry. When I descended the steps to the basement and flicked on the light, I immediately jumped backward (nearly falling over) when I saw a black object in front of me. It was just a suitcase that someone hadn't put away from a weekend family trip.

I mention all of this not only to acknowledge my own embarrassing capacity to freak myself out but also to suggest one possibility for what people experience when they encounter a ghostly presence. If a person admits that the existence of ghosts is possible—especially when she or he accepts the presence of a ghost in her or his life—mundane, everyday happenings can (and do) take on new meanings. In a class I teach on sexualities, I sometimes half-jokingly ask students to reflect on what it might be like to be a shoe salesman with a foot fetish; it is likely that the shoe buyer and that salesman experience the relatively mundane act of fitting shoes *quite* differently. It is possible that something similar is occurring with at least some of what informants reported in this study. By way of example, I have to admit that I've come to envy the people who reported having poltergeists in their home; they have a ready explanation for anything amiss in their household. Meanwhile, when something is missing or out of place in our home, Michele typically blames me—and often rightly so.

This may satisfy the skeptics. But unfortunately I'm still not telling the whole truth. Bear with me.

On the day in May 2013 that my university's Institutional Review Board approved this research, I met with a medium. I thought, "What better place to start than with someone who encounters ghosts routinely? Surely, a medium must be able to give me useful information, tips, insights, and pointers. I just need to gain her trust and confidence." I was right and I was wrong.

The medium, an elderly woman, graciously met with me. After probing deeply to be certain that I had no ill intent, she agreed to talk for a while. I told her all about the study—or, more accurately, what I *thought* the study was about at that time. She smiled kindly but was obviously uninterested in the sorts of questions I had. She did, however, tell me a lot about her experiences. She sees ghosts perpetually. She experiences a constant and shifting cast of mainly human but also some nonhuman spirits. Most are benign, some are friendly, a few are dangerous, and she gave me examples of her experiences with all three. She said she is sometimes called to help people rid their homes of an unwanted ghostly presence. She told me in detail about a particularly cantankerous presence—she called it a "void"—that she encountered in someone's home, which she said was powerful enough to knock her down and push her against a wall.

I was overwhelmed by what the medium said to me and struggled to stay focused while she was talking. I must have been staring at her at least half-blankly because, in my mind, I could not help but reflect on the first interview in Richard Mitchell's (2002) ethnography of survivalists. I felt that I had fallen into a similar self-inflicted trap, although unlike Mitchell, I wasn't secretly recording, and I'm glad to say that my informant did not have a gun pointed in my direction. But in all other respects, I was just as naïve and unprepared. It was a helpful reminder that reading about something doesn't necessarily bestow understanding. When it was time for me to depart, I left bewildered, a little scared of what I had gotten myself into, but grateful for the opportunity to begin a meaningful refinement of what, exactly, I intended to study about ghosts and hauntings. The medium then said something I will never forget: "Dennis, I must warn you [to] be careful. If you invite spirits, they may attach themselves or follow you." I didn't think much of her warning at the time but have since reflected on those words a lot.

I'm certain that most of the strange things I experienced are a product of my hyper-occupied mind, but not all of them. I'm still puzzled about how my wedding ring disappeared from my hand one night—I never take it off and feel naked without it. Even more perplexing, I cannot explain how, many hours later, the ring appeared on the floor, dead-center in the unusual step-up entry to my home office. I had been in and out of that room repeatedly, especially while I was frantically looking for the ring, and even if I was so distracted that I did not see it on the floor, it would have been impossible for me to pass it without stepping on or kicking it. In another incident, I heard a strange noise while sitting at my desk and turned to my right, where I saw my guitar case open and close on its own.

Most maddening of all, for a period of two months in the winter of 2014, I began openly speculating about a poltergeist that seemed to persistently take control of the cursor on my laptop. Once I felt a tingling electrical sensation as the cursor rapidly opened my e-mail and, in a matter of seconds, deleted all 126 messages, at least twenty of which were marked unread. Another time, the cursor moved rapidly to the upper right corner of the Word document in which I was transcribing an interview; again in a matter of seconds I watched helplessly as the cursor clicked "select all" and deleted all of the text, clicked the icon to close the document, and, when prompted to save the changes, chose "save." Multiple times my web browser opened on its own, the cursor flicking to a random image on the homepage and cutting and pasting the image to my desktop in the blink of an eye.[1] Like several of the people I spoke to in this research, I was greatly relieved when others witnessed these bizarre things happening with my computer, because those persistent experiences were starting to call my sanity into question. And they didn't end until I acknowledged the poltergeist and kindly asked it to stop.

These are just some of the uncanny things that occurred in the course of this research. I am convinced that most of them stemmed from hyperawareness brought on by perpetual thoughts of ghosts and hauntings—what Freud (2003 [1919]: 147) called an "omnipotence of thoughts." But I cannot dismiss all of them. That said, all of the uncanny events that I cannot dismiss as merely freaking myself out occurred only while I was devoting considerable time and intense thought to ghosts and hauntings. The apparition I witnessed in June 2013 appeared after hours of reflection on one particular ghost. I observed my guitar case open and close after several hours of writing about Allison's experiences with a ghost in her closet. The poltergeist haunting me through my computer appeared once I had set aside everything else in my life and devoted countless hours to the tedious task of transcribing interviews. Still, I must tell the truth: I cannot

---

1. Because my professional life is something I accomplish in, on, or through my computer, *nothing* can make me more anxious than someone, or something, that interferes with my ability to use my computer or my confidence in its fidelity. I've had a lot of nightmares in the course of this research, but none has been more terrifying than the prospect of inexplicably losing transcribed interviews, unpublished book manuscripts, or course materials that I have developed over the past two decades. If this was a poltergeist, it could not have chosen to haunt me in a more upsetting way.

explain these things that occurred. I cannot tell whether they were ghostly experiences. And I cannot say they were not.

GHOSTLY ABSENCES

> Ghosts often represent the things that words have not expressed or cannot express.
> —JUDITH RICHARDSON, *POSSESSIONS*

Writing a research manuscript is all about reporting the results of what was found in the study conducted. It is important, however, to pay at least some attention to what was not found—ghostly absences in the data—because what we do not see and hear is often just as significant and meaningful as what we do. In the course of this research, I did not see or hear a variety of things. Some I expected; others I did not. I comment on a few of the most significant absences here.

I did not see or hear from many men. The available literature consistently states that women are more likely to believe in and report experiences with ghosts (see Bader 2010; Bourque 1969; Greeley 1975; Lyons 2005; Newport and Strausberg 2001). Therefore, I expected to see and hear from more women than men, but not to the extent that I observed. Only seventeen men volunteered to report a ghostly encounter; women made up 76 percent of the total sample. Moreover, as previously mentioned, four people approached me with possible interest in sharing their ghostly experiences but chose not to participate in the study. While it is speculative, at best, to conclude anything about a sample of four, the gender distribution is the exact opposite: three of the four people who decided not to participate were men (75 percent). While we do not doubt that women are more likely to believe in ghosts, we also suggest that the greater willingness of women to *report* those experiences may be a significant variable to consider. It is reasonable to suggest that men may experience ghostly encounters more frequently than the available literature reports. They are simply less disposed to talk about it.

I did not see or hear from many Protestants. The participants in this study were from Minnesota, Iowa, North Dakota, South Dakota, and Wisconsin. This is a region of the United States in which, despite a sharp decline in religious affiliation across the country, a significant majority of the population identifies as Christian (Cooperman, Smith, and Ritchey 2015). An extensive study conducted by the Pew Research Center found that in these five states, 71–79 percent of the population identifies as Christian (Cooperman, Smith, and Ritchey 2015). Likewise, forty-five of the seventy-one participants in this study identified as Christian (63 percent), with twenty-two describing themselves as either "non-religious" or simply "spiritual" (31 percent). Moreover, the region is predominately Protestant; on average, more than half of the Christians in the five states of the study identify as Protestant, with fewer than one-quarter identifying as Catholic (Cooperman, Smith, and Ritchey 2015). In contrast, only twelve of the Christian participants in the study reported a Protestant religious background (17 percent). In an area of the country where Catholics make up less than a quarter of the religious population, the number of those who identified as Catholic or said they were raised Catholic was double that of those who identified as Protestant. Only four participants in the study self-identified as highly religious, and three of them were Catholic. Henry, for example, described himself not only as Catholic but also as "a very religious person." For him, the relationship between ghosts and Catholicism was implicit:

> For Catholics, the existence of ghosts is, in fact, a part of the informal doctrine of the church. The vernacular of the "Holy Ghost" kind of sets the stage, but apparitions have been a consistent part of the faith for at least four hundred years. I was raised in a Methodist household where all of this would have been viewed as superstition. But personal experience has taught me otherwise, regardless or because of the evolution of my religious and spiritual beliefs and practices.

Likewise, Roger Clarke's (2012) five-hundred-year history of ghosts illustrates the Catholic institutionalization of ghostly beliefs and experiences. "The Catholic Church rationalized (and to a large extent took over) the ancient belief in ghosts by teaching that such apparitions were the souls of those trapped in Purgatory, unable to rest until they have expiated their sins," Clarke (2012: 291) explains. With the early Protestant reformers denying Purgatory, the "question of whether one believed in ghosts now marked the difference between Catholic and Protestant as strongly as belief in transubstantiation of the host or the infallibility of the Pope. . . . No true Protestant could believe in ghosts" (Clarke 2012: 292–293). And, of course, Catholicism on the whole is a cosmology that is significantly cozier with the supernatural in general. Historically, Catholicism has had close associations with demons and divine intervention, saints and exorcists, degrees of miracles and combating witchcraft, to mention just a few.

Consistent with other literature (Bader, Mencken, and Baker 2010; Baker and Draper 2010), with few exceptions the people who volunteered to report their ghostly experiences in this study were moderately religious or spiritually flexible—and that was expected. Given the religious composition of the region, we expected and found that our informants mostly identified as Christians or said they were raised in Christianity, but not of the regular or devoted church-attending variety. But also, and equally because of the religious composition of the region, we did not expect that Catholics (and those who were raised Catholic) would make up the majority of the Christian participants in the study. The apparent affinity of Catholics for ghosts may be more than historical and may prove worthy of future research through use of larger samples and other methods of data collection and analysis.

I did not see or hear from many people reporting experiences with ghosts that had decidedly human characteristics. This absence surprised me the most. Ninety-eight of the 144 ghosts reported in this study (68 percent) had no observable human characteristics: they did not appear as apparitions that resembled people; nor did they communicate, speak, or otherwise vocalize in ways indicative of humanity. In everyday life, we interact on the basis of identified cues we glean from people in the ebb and flow of an ongoing information game that no one articulates better than Erving Goffman (1959). The exact opposite was the case in the vast majority of our study's reported ghostly encounters: the ghostly presence was defined not only by an uncanny happening but also by the absence of any identifying cues of humanity. As Judith Richardson (2003: 26) describes this condition, "Ghosts are habitually discerned and described in terms of vagueness, colorlessness, wispiness, incompleteness; they are most often recognized and defined precisely by their lack of definition or identifiers."

Thus, the reported experiences of the majority of the participants in this study were *presumed* to be the ghosts of former living people, but the informants did not report observations that confirmed the presence of something characteristically human. Poltergeists are a good example. Reported experiences with poltergeists almost universally involved a perceived presence that made itself known through inexplicable sounds and uncanny manipulation of objects in the environment. Sometimes participants reported experiences with poltergeists that included footsteps that were characteristically human, but otherwise, even if one accepts that these uncanny happenings were caused by a poltergeist, there was as much evidence to suggest that the presence was a formerly living person as a deceased cat, dog, or kangaroo.

In these instances, when people reported a ghostly encounter with a presumed former living person, whatever it was that they experienced was absent of human qualities and in that way uncannily *non*human. Unlike all people everywhere, these alleged ghosts were invisible, mute, nameless, genderless, and ageless; they had no race or ethnicity, social status, or other characteristics that are normatively associated with being a person.[2] Surely in these instances people experienced something inexplicable. But associating those strange happenings with the ghost of a former living person may be more a product of the application of stock cultural knowledge than anything directly related to the uncanny experience itself.

---

2. In ghost lore, folklorists have been able to examine interesting dynamics of characteristically human traits that appear in the ghost stories that people tell, especially aspects of race and gender. Thus, we originally anticipated adding our own analysis of these aspects of the experiences people report of ghostly encounters and were surprised that we collected insufficient data to do so. Moreover, in a region of the country with a long history of turbulent race relations with native populations, the absence of Native American ghosts in this study is especially noteworthy. Only two participants reported ghostly encounters that involved the spirits of deceased Native Americans or associations with Native American burial sites.

GHOSTLY GENRES

Throughout the pages of this book, I have focused on what can be called "everyday ghosts": the everyday uncanny experiences of upper midwestern Americans who believe they have experienced a ghostly presence. Early in the book, we suggested that "everyday ghosts" represent a unique genre of ghostly experiences, mainly because they exist outside the cultural authority and conventionalizing structures of religion and supernatural subcultures. In those everyday contexts, I have sought to illustrate how uncanny experiences become ghosts, the reasons people struggle with or against a will to believe, the variety and character of ghostly encounters, and the nested consequences of ghostly experiences. In this research, I encountered other genres of ghosts that we did not pursue—or, at least, did not include in the book—because they have unique characteristics that merit independent study. I conclude with a brief commentary on other genres worthy of investigation.

One significant genre of experiences not explored here consists of what I call "professionalized ghosts." Professionalized ghosts are subject to and at least partially understood within the discourses, practices, and technologies of mediums, paranormal investigators, and a "priesting" (Brady 1995) of the dead. If the people I spoke to are any indication of the general norm, it's reasonable to suggest that the majority of people do not seek professional help in response to their ghostly experiences. That said, it's equally apparent that some do, and more than likely for a wide variety of reasons. The professionals, in this case, are mediums, paranormal investigators, and religious authorities. One might superficially suggest that preexisting belief structures heavily influence which professional a person would consult for help on ghostly matters, with religious people consulting church authorities, supernatural enthusiasts consulting mediums, and those who prefer more concrete evidence calling on paranormal investigators. But that's far too simple. There are too many other contextual variables, including the nature of the ghostly encounter and, especially, the different services that the professionals offer. After all, if you wish to speak to or otherwise communicate directly with the spirits of the dead, a medium may be your only option; exorcizing a ghost requires religious authorities, and only paranormal investigators have the material technology (and patience) to gather empirical evidence of a haunting. Perhaps most interesting of all, while each of the ghostly professionals brings forth vastly different discourses for understanding, as well as practices and technology, in the end the professionalized ghost may very well emerge from similar dynamics and social forms.

In this study, I also ignored what I call "commercial ghosts." Commercial ghosts are found within establishments, even entire communities, that have vested economic interests in a reputation for being haunted. Haunted hotels and bed and breakfasts are among the most obvious and copious examples. As of June 2015, the website Haunted bnb.com listed 287 haunted bed and breakfasts in the United States alone. Haunted bed and breakfasts are identified for every state in the nation, although the market for commercial ghosts seems especially robust on the southern West Coast, with forty-six listed in California (seven in Oregon, and four in Washington). Some forms of "dark tourism" (Foley and Lennon 2000) equally benefit from commercial ghosts, and some literature explores the managerial and ethical issues that are involved with operating ghost tours (see Garcia 2012). Clearly, commercial ghosts have to be at least partly understood in the context of their literal capital, and their presence has to be at least partially foreshadowed by economic incentives. Indeed, "the business of ghosts has never been far away from the *business* of ghosts" (Clarke 2012: 286). Still, that doesn't explain why people pay for a ghost tour or an experience in any one of these countless establishments. Regardless, the obvious ways the phrase "most haunted" is used as a marketing slogan to attract business ought to be sufficient indication that commercial ghosts are a genre of their own.

"Institutional ghosts" are an extremely common genre of ghostly encounters—common enough to have partially appeared in portions of this book—and clearly merit significant independent investigation and analysis because of their unique and complex dynamics. Institutional ghosts not only haunt institutions (e.g., hospitals, churches, and schools) but also appear especially prevalent in places where people have been institutionalized (e.g., asylums, prisons, and orphanages). Institutional ghosts often appear as an ephemeral embodiment of profound human drama—pain, suffering, death, illness, disease, neglect, hopelessness, inhumane treatment. Perhaps most interesting of all, institutional ghosts are often deeply historical; they frequently haunt the architectural remains of bygone days when people lived different lives. As I found but did not include in this book, those historical institutional ghosts are often of once well-intended social reforms that resulted in tragic dumping grounds for the living human waste of society—orphanages, state schools for dependent and neglected children, asylums for the handicapped and insane—where people were subject to strict regimens, discipline, "moral training," or inhumane forms of "treatment" or, conversely, to neglect and unsanitary living conditions. For these reasons, historical institutional ghosts frequently reveal dark histories and a painful past and are riddled with a guilty collective memory. In these ways, institutional ghosts are especially promising to examine, not only for the significant ways they are "produced by the cultural and social life of the communities in which they appear" but also because these "hauntings demand deeper investigation because of what they reveal about how senses of the past and of place are apprehended and created, what they suggest about the marginal and invisible things that, for many recent scholars, texture and define identity, politics, and social life" (Richardson 2003: 3). For these reasons institutional ghosts ought to be especially fascinating for those who are most interested in understanding "history and biography and the relations between the two within society" (Mills 1959: 4).

A DOMYVIK IN
THE APARTMENT

Sofija was born in the Ukraine in 1992, where she lived her first twenty-one years of life. Eight months before our interview, Sofija had moved to the United States into an apartment where she and her roommates experienced a variety of uncanny happenings. "Recently my room-mates and I started noticing that things are not in the right place," Sofija said. "Things are not in the places where we put them before." She gave several examples:

> *One day, my roommate was cooking in the kitchen, and she had a dish and a cup on the table. She heard her phone ringing, so she went to answer it, and when she came back, the cup and dish [were] not on the table but on the floor in the exact same position as [they were] on the table, just now on the floor. . . . Another time my roommate had a Valentine's card from her boyfriend and she left it on the kitchen table. I looked at the card, then went back to my room to get something and out to the living room, and there was the card in the living room. I went to the kitchen table and the card was gone. Somehow the card moved from the kitchen table to the living room.*

Like some other experiences reported in this study, the ghost in Sofija's apartment sometimes meddles with the heating and cooling. "Another night, we turned on the heat because it's starting to get cold," Sofija said, "but, by the middle of the night it was just freezing." When she and her roommates woke up the next morning, they "found the thermostat had been turned off completely—and you can't easily turn it off, either. You have to press all these different buttons."

Sofija describes uncanny happenings that we would classify as clas-sic poltergeist activity, but that's not the word Sofija used to identify the ghost in her apartment. "We have a name for them [in my native language], and I was looking for a translation, but you don't have a name for that word," Sofija said. "But I called my friends back home, and they were, like, 'Yeah, for sure it's one of those.'"

I am especially curious about and interested in what Sofija is telling me. My entire paternal family is Ukrainian; my father immigrated to the United States at eleven, speaking nothing but Ukrainian. So I ask Sofija, "Can you pronounce for me very slowly what you call this spirit in your native language?" Sofija replies with careful enunciation, "dom-o-vick," graciously adding, "It's spelled d-o-m-y-v-i-k. My parents even told me about them, and they said it's all OK. We believe that these things are often in old buildings, and our apartment is pretty old. We accept it as tradition in my part of the Ukraine." She continued:

> Back in my home country when these kinds of things happen, we sprinkle some holy water on the walls so the evil can get out of our house. But it's also believed in my home country that some of these are actually good and helpful. So in order to have the friendly ones stay and the bad ones leave, you also put out some milk and some candies on the table. You then say some words, like, "Here you go. You can treat yourself."

Sofija responded to the domyvik in her apartment in accordance with the Ukrainian customs she had grown up with, and that seemed to resolve the problem. "After we did that, not much happened," Sofija claimed—or, at least, she and her roommates no longer experience anything irksome. "A couple times, doors would open and close, but not much, and we weren't afraid anymore. After that, everything became more peaceful."

Sofija grew up not only with a different word for the ghost in her apartment and not only with a different ritual for contending with it. She also grew up with a different set of beliefs about domyviks. In fact, as Sofija told me, "It's actually believed to be bad luck if your house doesn't have one":

> They are believed to be spirits that help keep your household clean, and, for example, if there are fights [among people living in the house], they will start to do weird stuff. I'm pretty sure it was something like that. . . . It's pretty regular, and especially in

my region of Ukraine. They are believed to be spirits from the woods, not to be feared, but the most important thing is not to have any arguments in the house and to treat them with a small dish of treats. It's just not that big a deal in the Ukraine. Very, very few people say they see one—but they can be heard and you can feel their presence.

Clearly, the uncanny happenings that Sofija attributed to the domyvik are indistinguishable from the kinds of activities many people in the study described to us of poltergeists. One might argue that Sofija simply has a different word in her native language to describe the same uncanny experiences. In other, more important respects, however, the domyvik that Sofija reported cannot be compared to the reported poltergeist experiences. Because of her cultural upbringing, Sofija thought about the domyvik differently from how others portrayed the poltergeists of their experiences. Domyviks are not presumed to be ghosts of former living people; they are, instead, "spirits from the woods." Sofija responded to the domyvik differently from how others reported dealing with a poltergeist. Sofija had a cultural ritual intended to rid her apartment of harmful domyviks and encourage the helpful and friendly ones to stay. The domyvik that Sofija reported functions differently from the poltergeists that others report. Unlike poltergeists that reportedly linger for no apparent reason or purpose, the domyvik encourages peaceful relationships: "weird" things happen only when there is turmoil, and the domyvik prefers tidiness and prompts serenity within the home (and all for the paltry price of a cup of milk and small bowl of candy).

Unlike the other experiences that fill the pages of this book, the ghostly encounter that Sofija reported to us was conventionalized by her Ukrainian upbringing. Consequently, Sofija's experiences are not comparable, or useful, for our analysis except to serve as an important contrast and reminder: all experiences of everyday life occur within taken-for-granted cultural frameworks of interpretation; the actions we take are structured by both explicit and subtle rituals; our beliefs emerge from a history of those interactions over time; and ghosts are as deeply saturated with culture as the words we speak, the clothing we wear, the food we eat, and other aspects of our everyday lives. In fact, the domyvik in the apartment is more overtly cultural than even Sofija is able to identify and describe—and perhaps in ways of which she is not even aware.

My third cousin Oksana Harasemiw is knowledgeable about all things Ukrainian and closely associated with scholars of Ukrainian heritage at the University of Manitoba. While she had never heard of a domyvik, she quickly figured out a highly significant association: folklore, like any aspect of culture, diffuses and adapts in a process of cultural transmission. The domyvik that Sofija described is one such manifestation of cultural diffusion. "It's actually spelled d-o-m-o-v-o-i," Oksana informed me. "It's rooted in Slavic folklore, but the word itself is from the Russian language." In Russian, domovoi literally means "from the house," and much like what Sofija describes, every house has one, according to Slavic folklore. The Slavic domovoi is regarded as a protector of the house and, if kept happy, maintains peace in the home and rewards its occupants by helping with chores. Also akin to what Sofija describes, in Slavic folklore to keep a domovoi happy one must leave him gifts—mainly milk and food.[1] Likewise, Slavic folklore warns that domovoi become angry when there is turmoil in the house and in those circumstance acts exactly like the poltergeists described in the pages of this book. Clearly, the uncanny happenings that Sofija described may not be explicable, but all other aspects of the spirit in her apartment are drenched in culture and steeped in tradition. Perhaps the same may be said of all ghostly encounters.

---

1. In Slavic folklore, domovoi are regarded as a male presence.

APPENDIX

Methods and Data

On the surface, there appear to be abundant sources for data on ghost-ly experiences. The Internet is especially plentiful, with websites that include many purported firsthand experiences with ghosts and haunt-ings. YourGhostStories.com allows registered users to submit their experiences anonymously, and as of June 2015 it included more than fifteen thousand sub-missions. Most handy of all, YourGhostStories.com provides a search engine for its extensive database of alleged ghostly encounters. GhostsofAmerica.com offers a similar and equally large database that is also searchable, and viewers can browse by geographic area, as well. Early in this research, I scanned these and other websites as a possible source for rich data. Unfortunately, I discov-ered several accounts of ghostly encounters at locations that do not exist, and that was sufficient to close the browser on growing concerns about the credibil-ity of sources where anonymous people report experiences to mass audiences. Undoubtedly, these websites are an extremely rich source for a vast amount of data. If appropriate permissions were obtained *and* qualifying statements were made about the credibility of the sources reporting the experiences, a fantastic study could be conducted.

Likewise, bookstores around the country frequently have "local interest" sections that contain volumes of regional ghost stories. Scanning several of these titles, I discovered published accounts that parallel some of the stories participants in this study reported. Ultimately, however, these texts do not cite sources, their stories are often sensationalized, and they're notoriously poor when it comes to fact-checking—especially (but not only) those that recount the legend of Loon Lake Cemetery. Sigmund Freud was correct when he wrote that the "uncanny that we find in fiction—in creative writing, imaginative literature—actually deserves to be considered separately." These literatures, he added, are "above all much richer than what we know from experience . . . *many things that would be uncanny if they occurred in real life are not uncanny in literature, and . . . in literature there are many opportunities to achieve uncanny effects that are absent in real life*" (Freud ([1919]: 155–156).

With the possible exception of Diane Goldstein's "Scientific Rationalism and Supernatural Experience Narratives" (2007), I am unaware of any empirical study that examines reported firsthand experiences with ghosts. Thus, I decided to rely on *only* firsthand reports from people willing to share those experiences with me directly. I was flexible, however, in how I collected the accounts and adjusted to the approach that was most comfortable for the informant. In the end, the data collected came from one or more of three sources: interviews, written accounts, and observations.

DATA COLLECTION AND ANALYSIS

Interviews were the most productive source of data. Michele and I conducted a total of forty-six interviews with fifty-two people who volunteered for this study. Some interviews were conducted in my office at Minnesota State University; others were conducted at informants' homes, coffee shops, or, when possible with appropriate permission, at the location where ghostly encounters were purported to occur. The interviews ranged from six minutes to more than ninety minutes, depending on the scope of the experience or experiences reported. In total, I recorded more than twelve hours of interview data.

As described in Chapter 1, early in this research I discovered problems with the use of the word "ghost." Roger Clarke (2012: 302) described the problem well when he wrote, "No one asks whether you have *heard* a ghost; people ask whether you have *seen* one." In other words, people most often associate ghosts with apparitions. Because the majority of reported ghostly encounters do not involve seeing a ghostly presence (at least not directly), the word "ghost" sometimes proved problematic. I quickly adopted a useful strategy to avoid this potential problem. After asking the usual demographic questions (e.g., age, occupation, highest level of education, racial or ethnic identity, and religious or spiritual beliefs), I started the main content of each interview with the same generic statement: "So, tell us what you experienced."

Aside from the demographics, I did not use any pre-set list of questions. The intent of each interview was to get the informant to talk about his or her experiences. "So, tell us what you experienced" proved highly effective in getting that conversation started. All subsequent questions were merely probes for additional information, to clarify things that I misunderstood, or to gather more information about things that had been stated vaguely. At the conclusion of interviews, informants often wanted to discuss the experiences they had reported, how they related to other reported experiences, and emerging key findings. These post-interview conversations were often quite lengthy, sometimes more than an hour. Informants were not only fascinated by how their experiences approximated the reported experiences of others but also, and just as often, comforted to learn that they were not the "only one."

All informants granted permission to digitally record interviews. Recorded interviews were handled with the customary security measures of qualitative research, as well as the normative tactics for ensuring confidentiality (e.g., the use of pseudonyms and omission of identifying information). I transcribed all of the interviews myself; no graduate students were harmed in the production of this book.

While I preferred to conduct interviews face to face, often traveling considerable distances to achieve that, busy schedules and remote locations occasionally necessitated other arrangements. Two interviews were conducted by phone, but by using a speaker phone, I was able to handle them the same way I conducted face-to-face interviews. One informant preferred to be interviewed via a series of e-mail exchanges and later agreed to meet with us at the location said to be haunted. One informant asked to have a few weeks to more fully document the ghostly occurrences in her life in a word-processing document that she later e-mailed to me; she also answered follow-up questions by e-mail.

Some interviewees provided lengthy accounts of complicated ghostly encounters. In other instances, especially those addressed in Chapter 4, the ghost stories people told resulted in significant consequences for them (or, at least, could do so). In those instances, I reconstructed what had been told to us in a narrative form that included additional data gathered from other sources and asked the interviewees to verify what I wrote for accuracy and to correct errors. This was especially important for the information we gathered about Loon Lake Cemetery. No one was allowed to read early drafts of our account until the facts had been thoroughly checked and approved by all invested parties—descendants of the Terwillegar family, the director of the Jackson County Historical Society, and especially Mary Chonko, whose efforts to combat the fictitious witch story and document the history of what has been destroyed have been painstaking and unequaled.

Some study participants preferred to write strictly about their ghostly experiences. I developed an open-ended qualitative survey to accommodate people who, for various reasons, didn't want to talk to me directly. The survey asked the same demographic questions and provided space for people to write about various kinds of ghostly experiences, including (1) personal encounters, (2) experiences reported to them by friends and family, and (3) localized legends. Nineteen participants in the study chose to complete the qualitative survey.

In all instances of participants who chose to write about their experiences, the surveys were completed in a word-processing document and returned electronically. Some participants who completed the qualitative survey agreed to answer follow-up questions, while many did not. The survey was moderately productive, but on the whole, the written accounts were generally short and left out important details. In cases in which we couldn't ask follow-up questions, the data were significantly less useful.

Field notes were taken throughout the study. These notes were a particularly important source of data for reconstructing information observed in our visits to places said to be haunted. During the interviews, I also frequently took immediate crude field notes as interviewees were speaking; after the interview concluded, those notes were expanded to include more detail. I listened carefully to what interviewees said but also observed body language and especially documented my observations of emotional responses. These notes were highly instrumental in reconstructing an ethnographic account that conveys the volatility and emotional intensity of some of the experiences that occurred. Because this is a reflexive ethnography, information reported by and observed among others was the central focus of data and analysis, which I merely *supplemented* with my experiences when appropriate or useful.

Data analysis followed the procedures of phenomenological research methods (Moustakas 1994: 118–119). Organization and analysis of data entail a process of (1) "horizonalizing" the data (i.e., "regarding every horizon or statement relevant to the topic and equation as having equal value"), (2) clustering units of meaning from the horizonalized data into common themes, (3) developing descriptions of experiences based on clusters of meaning units, and (4) integrating textual descriptions into the meanings—experiential and theoretical—of the phenomena studied.

SAMPLING AND THE SAMPLE

All seventy-one participants contacted us and agreed to volunteer for this study. All forty-six interviewees signed the customary informed consent, and for the one minor who participated in this study we obtained the appropriate permissions from legal guardians. For the surveys, a brief statement of purpose and contact information was provided at the top of the survey; otherwise, simply returning the survey constitutes what is called "implied consent" (i.e., if they didn't want to participate in the study, they would not have returned the survey).

For two years I announced the study in all of the courses I taught and, most gainfully, simply made it a point to mention the research as often possible in casual conversations with people in everyday life. Michele and I didn't go anywhere without at least consent forms and a digital recorder, since an opportunity for an interview could materialize from any conversation anywhere we went. Interviews most frequently came in delayed pairs where, at the conclusion, the interviewee would identify someone else in his or her life who had also had a ghostly experience that he or she might be willing to share. In these instances, I simply gave our contact information to the existing informant, and the additional contacts came to us. Since my university's Institutional Review Board currently disallows snowball sampling, and this study was severely crippled by that limitation,[1] the sampling method we used closely approximated snowball with one exception: I did not directly solicit participants in the study (they had to come to me, by institutional mandate).

The sample included fifty-four women and seventeen men. Ages ranged from sixteen to seventy-eight, with an average age of thirty-one. As we expected, given the racial and ethnic composition of the region, all but seven participants in this study are Caucasian. Some Hmong people agreed to volunteer, but for reasons discussed in Chapter 1 we could accept their generous offer only if they were not committed to traditional Hmong animist beliefs (in which ghosts are a common and conventionalized part of their spiritual belief system). Two Mexican Americans, two Asian Americans, one Hmong, and one mulatto represent the limited racial and ethnic diversity of the sample. The highest level of education ranged from tenth grade to a doctoral degree; on the whole, the sample is exceptionally well educated. Twenty-three of the seventy-one participants in the study have a bachelor's degree or higher (33 percent), and when we include those who reported at least "some college" education (including associate's degrees), the number jumps to sixty (85 percent).

USE OF PHOTOGRAPHS

Previous generations of ethnographers were limited in their ability to use photography proficiently because of the advanced technical skills necessary to produce high-quality images. Digital photography, however, has advanced to the point at which any ethnographer who does not go into the field with a camera in hand is lazy or oblivious to the potential. At the very least, photography makes field notes infinitely more efficient, since a series of photos can permanently record a vast amount of visual data, and switching the digital camera to video records all of the sounds and action, as well. Since the traditional goal of ethnography is the production of an up-close, intimate, and "thick" text, the use of photography in contemporary ethnography is as crucial to data collection as it is to re-presentation. Hundreds of photos were taken in the course of this study, and they were highly instrumental in creating ethnographic narratives that are richly descriptive.

In terms of re-presentation, visual methods—especially photography—are most evocatively used to capture action, particularly for scholars of the symbolic interactionist tradition. That is, photography is most evocative for data re-presentation when it captures people *doing* something. Portraits, landscapes, and images of inanimate objects are significantly less useful. However, if there is a way to capture people doing something with or among ghosts, I am not aware of it. Moreover, no ghosts volunteered to be interviewed, let alone gave me the opportunity to ask their permission to use photography, which presents an

---

1. How an Institutional Review Board can unilaterally disallow an entire method of data collection is perplexing, to say the least. `

interesting ethical dilemma: if a ghost did appear to me who was willing to talk and, let's further imagine, I was able to take its photograph, would I still need to obtain the requisite informed consent and permissions? If so, *how* would I do so?

The most common use of photography in data re-presentation is as documentation, because, as it is commonly understood, words are ideal for representation and images for presentation. Many of the images used in this book serve the usual documentary purpose: to show the reader material consequences and outcomes. This is especially evident in the images used in Chapter 4, where readers can see for themselves some of the destructive consequences of the fictitious witch legend of Loon Lake Cemetery. In that chapter, we also use photographs we took at Framton Cemetery to illustrate opposite outcomes. Those photographs not only document, but through contrast they also visually supplement the main argument of the chapter. In these documentary uses of photography, we also frequently added titles and captions beneath the images to provide additional information about the main subject to help readers better contextualize what they are seeing. Titles and captions were unnecessary in most other uses of photographs in this book because the accompanying text adequately contextualizes the images that are seen.

Other images used in the book are intended purely to create a dramatic effect. Occasionally, readers will encounter an artfully captured, full-page photo of a mundane object that, through the control of information in the text, is later redefined in a manner that closely approximates the experiences that were reported to us and reconstructed in narrative form. For example, the mundane old chimney in the attic (see "Ghostly Genesis") is something Tara sees with new eyes since she discovered a chilling and mysterious confession of a murder that allegedly occurred on it. Likewise, we sought to create a similar effect for the reader: the photograph of the chimney that the reader first sees in "Ghostly Genesis" cannot be seen the same way at the conclusion of the narrative.

Finally, some images are intended simply to artfully illustrate an idea that is articulated with words. In "If the Walls Could Talk (or Sing)," we comment briefly on the parallels between ghosts and contemporary smartphones. The image that we carefully created that appears on the cover of this book simply expresses those reflections visually.

We cannot be certain whether these various uses of photography are effective. Critics and time will be the judge. Still, we believe the creative risk is worth the possible consequences either way. I took all of the photographs in the book, and for the record, I don't consider myself a skilled photographer. That said, I don't consider myself a novelist or poet, either, but I still write.

ETHICAL CONSIDERATIONS

Research on ghosts and hauntings needs to carefully deliberate multiple serious ethical considerations. Just because the ghost is presumed to be a former living person does not mean that harm cannot be done to the dead. Descendants of the dead must also be protected from any possible harm associated with the research. Living people who report experiences with ghosts may be stigmatized, and properties associated with hauntings may be subject to unwanted attention, damage, or devaluation. Reports of ghostly encounters may entail recounting frightening events that can be traumatizing or intensely grief-laden or otherwise concern emotional subjects that are difficult for people to talk about. These were all serious issues throughout this study and commanded constant attention in my effort to conduct this research with the greatest ethical integrity.

With most qualitative research, the main potential for harm lies not in the processes of collecting data but, rather, in *reporting* the information gathered. As long as we abide by the principles of informed consent, and we clearly emphasize to informants that they can withdraw from the study at any time and do not have to answer questions if they don't want to, the potential for harm is very low when people merely talk about their beliefs and experiences. For the most part, this book is no exception—but with one caveat: it was not uncommon for people to speak about experiences that are at least mildly traumatizing or emotionally sensitive. In most instances, these were brief moments in the interviews in which the respondents were able to quickly regain composure and thus were not unlike other times when they talked about those experiences for non-research purposes. Normative degrees of acknowledging these emotions and expressed compassion were sufficient in most cases. Only twice did we observe an excessive level of discomfort: one respondent showed signs of extreme anxiety, and another showed signs of extreme grief. In both instances, we stopped the interview and reminded the informants that they didn't have to speak about these things if they didn't want to and could withdraw from the study if the experience was too uncomfortable. In neither instance did the informant take that option.

The normative procedures of ensuring confidentiality—the use of pseudonyms, as well as the omission or changing of identifying information—are just as crucial to studies of experiences with ghosts and hauntings as any other context for research. Only a few participants in this study are open about their ghostly experiences. Most are guarded about who they will speak to and fully aware that their stories could result in ridicule or stigmatization. One person contacted me with an exceptional experience that I was extremely interested in including, but no amount of assurance of confidentiality was sufficient; he was deeply concerned about not only the potential stigma of having reported a ghostly experience if he was inadvertently outed but also its potentially catastrophic effects on his career (and for good reason, given his occupation). Clearly, those who intend to study people's experiences with ghosts and hauntings must treat all potentially identifying information with the highest level of confidentiality.

One person contacted me about extraordinary occurrences within his home and, once again, no amount of assurance of confidentiality was sufficient. In his case, the primary concern was not his own reputation but the potential for unwanted attention to, and devaluation of, his property if the location of his home were inadvertently revealed. His concern is quite valid. With the exception of commercial enterprises that capitalize on either a reputation for being haunted or the presence of what I call a "commercial ghost," a haunted house is a financial liability. Homes believed to be haunted fall into a category that relators call "stigmatized properties"; they are known to take longer to sell and sell at lower prices than comparable homes (see Christie 2001). Furthermore, places that are believed to be haunted attract unwanted attention; several accounts in this book describe locations that informants visited for no reason other than that the places had a reputation for being haunted—and those visits occasionally entailed vandalism and other forms of property damage.

As these examples illustrate, ethical research on ghosts and hauntings must protect the confidentiality not only of people but also of *places* believed to be haunted. I achieved that objective in three ways. First, I collected data over as wide a geographic area as I could; even given time and budget constraints, the travel for this research amounted to more than five thousand miles. Second, these locations are reported using only general descriptors (e.g., "a small rural midwestern town"). Last, while we sometimes report architectural and historical details of the places we visited, that information was omitted when describing such features that had the potential to make the locations identifiable. For one location in particular, we omitted all references to its unique history and architecture because it is highly unlikely that there is another place like it anywhere in the U.S. Midwest.

Given the study's relatively large geographic area, use of highly general descriptors, and omission of unique identifying features, I am sure that the locations of the places we visited have been kept in confidence. No study participant allowed us to visit his or her home or other private property without this assurance, and we extended that same ethical commitment to abandoned and public locations. Loon Lake Cemetery is the only exception, and the decision to reveal its location was made in consultation with all invested parties, who all agreed that doing so has more potential to bring positive outcomes than harmful ones.

Finally, research on ghosts and hauntings must be attentive to protecting the reputation of the dead, as well as the privacy, wishes, and emotions of their living descendants. Some of our informants reported ghostly encounters that they relate to tragic accidents or fatal mistakes of someone in the community. In these instances, even though the fatalities are a matter of public record, we chose not to disclose names of the deceased or exact details about their deaths. Like the unwanted attention that can be brought to a location believed to be haunted, ghostly encounters that are associated with tragic accidents and fatal mistakes can bring unwanted attention to an unfortunate event, as well as to grieving families and friends left behind.

REFERENCES

Ascher, Robert. 1999. "Tin Can Archaeology." In *Material Culture Studies in America*, ed. Thomas Schlereth, 325–337. Walnut Creek, CA: Altamira Press.

Asma, Stephan. 2009. *On Monsters: An Unnatural History of Our Worst Fears*. New York: Oxford University Press.

Bader, Christopher, F. Carson Mencken, and Joseph Baker. 2010. *Paranormal America: Ghost Encounters, UFO Sightings, Bigfoot Hunts, and Other Curiosities in Religion and Culture*. New York: New York University Press.

Baker, Joseph, and Scott Draper. 2010. "Diverse Supernatural Portfolios: Certitude, Exclusivity, and the Curvilinear Relationship between Religiosity and Paranormal Beliefs." *Journal for the Scientific Study of Religion* 49 (3): 413–424.

Baskin, Wade. 1972. *The Dictionary of Satanism*. New York: Philosophical Library.

Bennett, Gillian. 1999. *Alas Poor Ghost! Traditions of Belief in Story and Discourse*. Logan: Utah State University Press.

Bergland, Renee. 2000. *The National Uncanny: Indian Ghosts and American Subjects*. Hanover, NH: Dartmouth College Press.

Bourque, Linda. 1969. "Social Correlates of Transcendental Experiences." *Sociological Analysis* 30 (3): 151–163.

Brady, Erika. 1995. "Bad Scares and Joyful Hauntings: 'Priesting' the Supernatural Predicament." In *Out of the Ordinary: Folklore and the Supernatural*, ed. Barbara Walker, 145–158. Logan: Utah State University Press.

Bultmann, Rudolf. 1953. "A Reply to the Theses of J. Schniewind." In *Kerygma and Myth: A Theological Debate*, ed. Hans Werner Bartsch, trans. Reginald Fuller, 4–5. London: SPCK.

CBS News. 2012. "Best Haunted Graveyard in Minnesota," October 27. Available at http://minnesota.cbslocal.com/top-lists/the-best-haunted-graveyards-in-minnesota. Accessed April 23, 2013.

Chonko, Mary. 2013. *Loon Lake Cemetery*. Jackson, MN: Livewire Printing.

Christie, Les. 2001. "Real Estate's Scary Side: Three Beds, Two Baths, One Ghost, a Haunting Tale." *CNN Money* 31:1–4.

Clarke, Roger. 2012. *Ghosts: A Natural History: 500 Years of Searching for Proof*. New York: St. Martin's Press.

Collison-Morley, Lacy. 2009. *Greek and Roman Ghost Stories*. Charleston, SC: BiblioLife.

Cooperman, Alan, Gregory Smith, and Katherine Ritchey. 2015. "America's Changing Religious Landscape: Christians Decline Sharply as Share of Population." Pew Research Center. Available at http://www.pewforum.org/files/2015/05/RLS-05-08-full-report.pdf. Accessed June 2015.

Durkheim, Émile. 1915. *The Elementary Forms of Religious Life*. New York: Free Press.

Ellis, Bill. 1993. "Adolescent Legend-Tripping." *Psychology Today* 17:68–69.

Emmons, Charles, and Jeff Sobal. 1981. "Paranormal Beliefs: Testing the Marginality Hypothesis." *Sociological Focus* 14 (1): 49–56.

Foley, Malcolm, and John Lennon. 2000. *Dark Tourism: The Attraction of Death and Disaster*. Independence, KY: Cengage Learning.

Fox, John. 1992. "The Structure, Stability, and Social Antecedents of Reported Paranormal Experiences." *Sociological Analysis* 53 (4): 417–431.

Freud, Sigmund. 2003 (1919). *The Uncanny*. New York: Penguin.

Friedlander, Michael. 1995. *At the Fringes of Science*. Boulder, CO: Westview.

Gallup Organization. 2005. "Americans' Belief in Psychic and Paranormal Phenomena Is up over Last Decade." Available at http://www.gallup.com/poll/4483/Americans-Belief-Psychic-Paranormal-Phenomena-Over-Last-Decade.aspx. Accessed October 4, 2013.

Garcia, Beatriz. 2012. "Management Issues in Dark Tourism Attractions: The Case of Ghost Tours in Edinburgh and Toledo." *Journal of Unconventional Parks, Tourism, and Recreation Research* 4 (1): 14–19.

Gilovich, Thomas. 1991. *How We Know What Isn't So: The Fallibility of Human Reason in Everyday Life*. New York: Free Press.

Glock, Charles, and Rodney Stark. 1965. *Religion and Society in Tension*. Chicago: Rand McNally.

Goffman, Erving. 1959. *Presentation of Self in Everyday Life*. New York: Anchor.

Goldstein, Diane. 2007. "Scientific Rationalism and Supernatural Experience Narratives." In *Haunting Experiences: Ghosts in Contemporary Folklore*, ed. Diane Goldstein, Sylvia Grider, and Jeannie Thomas, 60–78. Logan: Utah State University Press.

Goldstein, Diane, Sylvia Grider, and Jeannie Thomas. 2007. *Haunting Experiences: Ghosts in Contemporary Folklore*. Logan: Utah State University Press.

Goode, Erich. 2000. *Paranormal Beliefs: A Sociological Approach*. Prospect Heights, IL: Waveland.

Gordon, Avery. 1997. *Ghostly Matters: Hauntings and the Sociological Imagination*. Minneapolis: University of Minnesota Press.

Greeley, Andrew. 1975. *The Sociology of the Paranormal: A Reconnaissance*. Beverly Hills, CA: Sage.

Harris, Paul. 2000. *The Work of the Imagination*. Oxford: Blackwell.

Hoff, Eva. 2004–2005. "A Friend Living inside Me: The Forms and Functions of Imaginary Companions." *Imagination, Cognition and Personality* 24 (2): 151–189.

Holstein, James, and Jaber Gubrium. 2000. *The Self We Live By: Narrative Identity in a Postmodern World*. New York: Oxford University Press.

Hufford, David. 1995. "Beings without Bodies: An Experience-Centered Theory of the Beliefs in Spirits." In *Out of the Ordinary: Folklore and the Supernatural*, ed. Barbara Walker, 11–45. Logan: Utah State University Press.

James, William. 1905. *The Principles of Psychology*, vol. 1. New York: Henry Holt.

Jones, Louis. 1944. "The Ghosts of New York: An Analytical Study." *Journal of American Folklore* 57 (226): 237–254.

———. 1959. *Things That Go Bump in the Night*. Syracuse, NY: Syracuse University Press.

Kalish, Richard, and David Reynolds. 1973. "Phenomenological Reality and Postdeath Contact." *Journal for the Scientific Study of Religion* 12 (2): 209–221.

Kurtz, Paul. 1991. *The Transcendental Temptation: A Critique of Religion and the Paranormal*. Buffalo, NY: Prometheus.

Lamont, Peter. 2013. *Extraordinary Beliefs: A Historical Approach to a Psychological Problem*. Cambridge: Cambridge University Press.

Leiserowitz, Anthony, Edward Maibach, Connie Roser-Renouf, Geoff Feinberg, and Peter Howe. 2012. "Climate Change in the American Mind: American's Global Warming Beliefs and Attitudes in September, 2012." Report. Yale Project on Climate Change, New Haven, CT.

Lett, James. 1992. "The Persistent Popularity of the Paranormal." *Skeptical Inquirer*, Summer, 381–388.

Lipsitz Bem, Saundra. 1993. *The Lenses of Gender: Transforming the Debate on Sexual Inequality*. New Haven, CT: Yale University Press.

Lyng, Stephen. 1990. "Edgework: A Social Psychological Analysis of Voluntary Risk-Taking." *American Journal of Sociology* 95 (4): 851–886.

Lyons, Linda. 2005. "Paranormal Beliefs Come (Super)Naturally to Some." *Gallup*, November 1. Available at http://www.gallup.com/poll/19558/Paranormal-Beliefs-Come-SuperNaturally-Some.aspx. Accessed October 2, 2013.

MacDonald, William. 1994. "The Popularity of Paranormal Experiences in the United States." *Journal of American Culture* 17 (3): 35–42.

———. 1995. "The Effects of Religiosity and Structural Strain on Reported Paranormal Experiences." *Journal for the Scientific Study of Religion* 34 (3): 366–376.

Majors, Karen. 2013. "Children's Perceptions of Their Imaginary Companions and the Purposes They Serve: An Exploratory Study in the United Kingdom." *Childhood* 20 (4): 550–565.

Mead, George. 1934. *Mind, Self, and Society*. Chicago: University of Chicago Press.

Meltzer, Bernard. 2003. "Mind." In *Handbook of Symbolic Interactionism*, ed. Larry Reynolds and Nancy Herman-Kinney, 253–266. New York: Rowman and Littlefield.

Mencken, F. Carson, Christopher Bader, and Ye Jung Kim. 2009. "Round Trip to Hell in a Flying Saucer: The Relationship between Conventional Christian and Paranormal Beliefs in the United States." *Sociology of Religion* 70 (1): 65–85.

Mills, C. Wright. 1959. *The Sociological Imagination*. New York: Oxford University Press.

Mitchell, Richard. 2002. *Dancing at Armageddon: Survivalism and Chaos in Modern Times*. Chicago: University of Chicago Press.

Moran, Mark, and Mark Sceurman. 2005. *Weird U.S.: Your Travel Guide to America's Local Legends and Best Kept Secrets*. New York: Sterling.

Moustakas, Clark. 1994. *Phenomenological Research Methods*. Thousand Oaks, CA: Sage.

Newport, Frank, and Maura Strausberg. 2001. "Americans' Belief in Psychic and Paranormal Phenomena Is up over Last Decade." Gallup News Service.

Orenstein, Alan 2002. "Religion and Paranormal Belief." *Journal for the Scientific Study of Religion* 42:301–312.

Pearson, D., H. Rouse, S. Doswell, C. Ainsworth, O. Dawson, K. Simms, L. Edwards, and J. Faulconbridge. 2001. "Prevalence of Imaginary Companions in a Normal Child Population." *Child: Care, Health and Development* 27:13–22.

Pimple, Kenneth. 1995. "Ghosts, Spirits, and Scholars: The Origins of Modern Spiritualism." In *Out of the Ordinary: Folklore and the Supernatural*, ed. Barbara Walker, 75–89. Logan: Utah State University Press.

Puckett, Newbell. 1931. "Religious Folk Beliefs of Whites and Negros." *Journal of Negro History* 16:9–35.

Rice, Tom. 2003. "Believe It or Not: Religious and Other Paranormal Beliefs in the United States." *Journal for the Scientific Study of Religion* 42 (1): 95–106.

Richardson, Judith. 2003. *Possessions: The History and Uses of Haunting in the Hudson Valley*. Cambridge, MA: Harvard University Press.

Seiffge-Krenke, Inge. 1993. "Close Friendships and Imaginary Companions in Adolescence." *New Directions for Child Development* 60 (1): 73–87.

———. 1997. "Imaginary Companions in Adolescence: A Sign of a Deficient or Positive Development?" *Journal of Adolescence* 20 (2): 137–154.

Shermer, Michael. 1997. *Why People Believe Weird Things: Pseudo-science, Superstition, and Bogus Notions of Our Time*. New York: W. H. Freeman.

Sparks, Glenn. 2001. "The Relationship between Paranormal Beliefs and Religious Beliefs." *Skeptical Inquirer*, September–October, 50–56.

Stenger, Victor. 1990. *Physics and Psychics: The Search for a World beyond the Senses*. Buffalo, NY: Prometheus.

Synnott, Anthony. 1993. *The Body Social: Symbolism, Self and Society*. New York: Routledge.

Taylor, Marjorie, Stephanie Carlson, Bayta Maring, Lynn Gerow, and Carolyn Charley. 2004. "The Characteristics and Correlates of Fantasy in School-Age Children: Imaginary Companions, Impersonation, and Social Understanding." *Developmental Psychology* 40 (6): 1173–1187.

Thomas, Jeannie. 2007a. "The Usefulness of Ghost Stories." In *Haunting Experiences: Ghosts in Contemporary Folklore*, ed. Diane Goldstein, Sylvia Grider, and Jeannie Thomas, 25–59. Logan: Utah State University Press.

———. 2007b. "Gender and Ghosts." In *Haunting Experiences: Ghosts in Contemporary Folklore*, ed. Diane Goldstein, Sylvia Grider, and Jeannie Thomas, 81–110. Logan: Utah State University Press.

Thomas, Keith. 1971. *Religion and the Decline of Magic*. New York: Scribner's.

Thomas, W. I., and Dorothy Thomas. 1928. *The Child in America: Behavior Problems and Programs*. New York: Knopf.

Tobacyk, Jerome, and Gary Milford. 1983. "Belief in Paranormal Phenomena: Assessment Instrument Development and Implications for Personality Functioning." *Journal of Personality and Social Psychology* 44:1029–1037.

Truzzi, Marcello. 1971. "Definitions and Dimensions of the Occult: Towards a Sociological Perspective." *Journal of Popular Culture* 5 (3): 635–646.

Tucker, Elizabeth. 2005. "Ghosts in Mirrors: Reflections of the Self." *Journal of American Folklore* 118 (468): 186–203.

———. 2007. *Haunted Halls: Ghostlore of American College Campuses*. Jackson: University Press of Mississippi.

Turner, Victor. 1969. *The Ritual Process: Structure and Anti-structure*. Chicago: Aldine Transaction.

Van Gennep, Arnold. 1961. *The Rites of Passage*. Chicago: University of Chicago Press.

Vannini, Phillip, Dennis Waskul, and Simon Gottschalk. 2011. *The Senses in Self, Society, and Culture: A Sociology of the Senses*. New York: Routledge.

Walker, Barbara, ed. 1995. *Out of the Ordinary: Folklore and the Supernatural*. Logan: Utah State University Press.

Wallace, Anthony. 1966. *Religion: An Anthropological View*. New York: Random Books.

Warner, Marina. 1998. *No Go the Bogeyman: Scaring, Lulling, and Making Mock*. New York: Farrar, Straus and Giroux.

Waskul, Dennis. 2002. "The Naked Self: Being a Body in Televideo Cybersex." *Symbolic Interaction* 25 (2): 199–227.

———. 2009. "The Importance of Insincerity and Inauthenticity for Self and Society: Honesty Is Not the Best Policy." In *Authenticity in Culture, Self, and Society*, ed. Phillip Vannini and Patrick Williams, 51–64. Hampshire, UK: Ashgate.

———. 2015. "Going to the Bathroom." In *Popular Culture as Everyday Life*, ed. Dennis Waskul and Phillip Vannini, 145–154. New York: Routledge.

Waskul, Dennis, and Phillip Vannini. 2008. "Smell, Odor, and Somatic Work: Sense-Making and Sensory Management." *Social Psychology Quarterly* 71 (1): 53–71.

Waskul, Dennis, Phillip Vannini, and Desiree Wiesen. 2007. "Women and Their Clitoris: Personal Discovery, Signification, and Use." *Symbolic Interaction* 30 (2): 151–174.

Wren-Lewis, John. 1974. "Resistance to the Study of the Paranormal." *Journal of Humanistic Psychology* 14 (2): 41–48.

Wuthnow, Robert. 1978. *Experimentation in American Religion.* Berkeley: University of California Press.

Zimbardo, Philip. 2008. *The Lucifer Effect: Understanding How Good People Turn Evil.* New York: Random House.

INDEX

Dennis Waskul is a Professor of Sociology and Distinguished Faculty Scholar at Minnesota State University, Mankato, and former president of the Society for the Study of Symbolic Interaction. He has authored, co-authored, or edited a variety of books, including *Body/Embodiment* (with Phillip Vannini), *The Senses in Self, Society, and Culture* (with Phillip Vannini and Simon Gottschalk), and *Popular Culture as Everyday Life* (edited with Phillip Vannini).

Michele Waskul is an independent scholar with a focus on special education.